Buddhist Mandalas:
Explore Parallel Realities
with
Sacred Geometry

Book 1

VON D. GALT

All rights reserved. This book, or ebook, or parts thereof may not be reproduced in any form, stored in a retrieval system, or transmitted in any form by any means – electronic, mechanical, photocopy, recording, or otherwise – without prior written consent and permission of the author except in the case of brief quotations in articles and reviews as provided by the United States of America copyright law.

While the author has made every effort to provide accurate information at the time of publication, neither the publisher nor the author assumes responsibilities for errors or for changes that occur after publication.

Please, consider requesting that your local library branch purchase a copy of this book.

ISBN: 9781516947980

Cover designed and book written by Vongphet Douangphrachanh Galt during shelter-at-home in Seattle, WA during the Covid-19 pandemic.

Kwan Yin artwork by Fabiana Trere who drew it while in quarantine lock-down in Milan, Italy during the Covid-19 pandemic.

Copyright © 2020 Von D. Galt

Dedicated to my daughter, Samsara Belle Galt, and my son, Richard Enso Galt. My children inspire me to document my lifelong knowledge of spirituality from my family tradition of Buddhism. I am grateful to experience joy through my daughter's zest for life, and I'm very grateful to have my son. He manifested through after the miscarriages of both my angel babies, Bodhi and Dharma. As a dear Bodhisattva, *I surrender* back *to the void* and live in gratitude for the Lord giving me the ability to serve dharma talks in the age of consciousness with the eternal support of my dear husband, James Evan McCanless Galt. I am truly blessed. Whatever tradition brought you to your awakening and ascension, thank you for being open-minded to Buddhism. A spiritual approach to life is the way of the Buddha and is a harmonious companion with *many traditions*. Lastly, thank you, Metatron, Kwan Yin, and Yeshuah, for laying out the research one at a time through synchronicity so that this book can be written. I wish everyone many abundant blessings in whatever parallel reality you explore along your sojourn back home.

CONTENTS

Introduction 1
Chapter 1: What is Sacred Geometry? 14
    Sacred Geometry in Earth's Grid 24
    Sacred Space & Ley Lines 48
    Vesica Piscis 65
    Flower of Life Research Leads to Metatron's Cube. 77
    Flower of Life in Language Changes DNA 87
    Metatron's Cube 103
Chapter 2: Sacred Geometry in Spirituality 125
    Sri Yantra 131
    Yin Yang Symbol 165
    Tree of Life 183
    Torus Vortex 199
    Swastika in Indigenous Cultures 213
Chapter 3: What is Consciousness? 232
    Consciousness & Oneness 240
    Power of the Heart 260
    Meditation Changes Reality 289
    Awakening & Ascension 321
Conclusion 355
About the Author 373
Index 374
Bibliography 375

Introduction

"There are only two mistakes one can make along the road to truth; not going all the way, and not starting."
—Siddhartha Gautama, 1st Buddha

Buddhism speaks about your reality as a reflection of your personal vibration. The spiritual tradition talks much about grounding yourself and working out those skeletons in your closet so you can transmute them back into joy and live in the reality that fits your vibration. Any unbalanced energy, otherwise commonly referred to as "karma" in Buddhism, can be reset through the path of awakening to the greater reality and becoming a conscious creator of your own life. There are also good karma merits that are attained and distributed in your incarnations. However, the Buddha will do things out of his or her good nature without needing any form of payment. Everyone can attain their Buddha-nature because their destiny is mastery of their dominion. Discord in all realities is the pressure that helps mold you into a stronger person having lived through it. How you handle that pressure is a mirror of yourself.

This is all a very realistic holographic reality, and it is testing you to allow you to grow from it. Be grateful for mini experiences that test your character, which layer on top of one another instead of extreme polarizing experiences. This is grace experienced and realized. The Buddhist tradition speaks about how you choose all of this, the triumphs and the pitfalls beforehand, and then you forgot the memory to see if you really can pass your test without this knowledge or will you make the same mistakes. Lucid dreaming, meditation, contemplation, and hypnosis are some tools that offer insights into the intent behind your pre-incarnation life plans. Unlike other realms, Earth is an experience where everyone is leveled at an equal setting by incarnating without prior residual memory. The good guys, the bad guys, the in-betweens are all characters in a play. The Lord is more loving than many people give credit to. You choose to play for rapid development.

In Buddhism, there are no punishments, just a life review to see if you learned, grew, or need to repeat the lesson over again. Lombardo, hell, these are self-manifested realities for punishment that is nowhere close to the regrets your soul feels long after the body perishes. Since everything in creation is expressions of polarity, there is a Lombardo. However, very few souls will ever experience it. It is experienced if someone chooses to experience Lombardo instead of completing a life review and working with the spirit world to address their incarnations' effects. *Your consciousness is the cause, and the reflection is the effect. Simple cause and effect.*

If someone doesn't want to go to the spirit world, they do not have to. Even in Lombardo, when a soul decides they had enough of the pain and suffering in Lombardo, in a split second, they are in the spirit world with everyone else. So, lifetime after lifetime, many Buddhists believe we reincarnate to make right the mistakes we regret while trying *not* to create new regrets and imbalances in our relationships.

Many other souls incarnate into Earth for other reasons as well. Some incarnations are here to experience what the Earth has to offer, and it is not all to learn different lessons for personal expansion. Think of these other souls as tourists. Incarnating as a human on Earth is not the only game to choose from in all of creation. However, souls play the games appropriate to their level of attunement.

All experiences, even positive ones, contribute to personal expansion. There are many reasons why souls choose the Earth incarnation to experience. As a Buddhist, I ask what the lesson is and what the takeaway is from this experience. That's where I see the playbook. *In the Buddhist tradition, you must keep in mind, that there are parallel realities, parallel outcomes to events, and there are parallel people.* It's been mathematically proven by our physicists that parallel realities exist, but it isn't easy to prove while you are living in one.

Residual memory is what is left when traveling between parallel realities. There is no right or wrong way to travel between parallel realities using your Merkabah. It comes down to the personal choice of how someone wants to experience parallel realities based on the perspectives and actions that they project outwards into the reality they exist in at the time.

From moment to moment, we are shifting our perception of reality based on our personal resonance.

Everything is a mirror. People are your mirrors. The demanding situations brought out on the table are that many repressed unresolved issues are hiding inside many people's hearts. How you handle your life experiences is what determines your spiritual growth. Your experiences and spirituality is the only thing that passes with you upon death. Everything in life is spiritual lessons. You don't get to check in on Sunday and check out the rest of the week. You have to do the work to get the most of your current incarnation. These repressed unresolved issues are what spewed out from you on to others when you blatantly call people horrible names and insults, regardless of any consequences to protect your ego.

Love, logic, it's been thrown out the window and replaced with survival instincts. It mirrors the anger and rage inside that needs to be worked through to uncover the belief you have about yourself for why you feel the way you do regarding anything. That anger and hate are what is manifesting your reality. If you have hate in your heart and you seek revenge, then you will manifest a reality where you attract more of the same kind of experiences over and over again until you learn not to re-create it.

If you recognize and transmute that hatred, then the parallel version of people and events that keeps coming forth will become more neutral to more preferable. This is how your vibrational frequency based on your current level of consciousness picks timelines. Your consciousness has a resonance much like the Earth's Schumann resonance, which has an energy level.

Much like all energy, the more strength a body of energy is, the more effect its field has on the surrounding environment. Every decision you make is spiritual and propels you into the appropriate parallel reality. Yes, this is a book about awakening with sacred geometry. However, to truly understand sacred geometry, one will also understand the metaphysics of consciousness inside themselves, which functions as a navigation tool. Your consciousness is the compass that activates that black hole inside your Merkabah, and shifts you into a parallel reality. There will be Buddhist insights from my understanding of metaphysics, which provides a baseline for fully grasping the nature of sacred geometry in your direct experience of the reality you exist in now.

As you read each chapter, you are reading the original research I conducted about the topic discussed. Each topic supports each other through the articles that follow it afterward. By the end of the book, you will get an understanding of sacred geometry and how it symbolizes the relationship of people's energetic mandala as seen in much Buddhist artwork and how consciousness factors into the perfection of your mandala. Through getting a glimpse of the metaphysic and consciousness research in these various topics I choose to write about, you will see the meaning of Buddhist mandalas.

You should fully understand how every Buddhist mandala represents different Buddhist teachers. Buddhas are a term in Buddhism to refer to a person who has awakened to the greater reality of our holographic universe. They are *regular people* who attained Buddhahood by having their spiritual awakening and ascending their consciousness level into becoming an avatar, which is riding in their energetic mandala.

I aim to successfully explain that all sacred geometry seen in many religious and spiritual artworks worldwide is the same thing. When I explain how all the various interpretations support one another, you will see that all spiritual traditions try to explain the meaning conveyed in Buddhist mandala artwork. Everyone is sacred geometry traveling through multiple parallel realities in their level of consciousness.

Study the Buddhist mandala artwork in this book over and over again. You will see the truth of the sages. There are people at different levels of consciousness all over the universe working towards their awakening and ascension to attain Buddhahood at some point in their exploration of parallel universes. Each house presents different realities, which all go about their own stories in the cosmos. *Each dominion or dimensional reality has various Buddhas exploring it and, along the way, offer dharma talks about enlightenment to those who seek it.*

For others, they will carry on their story in that reality as part of their process towards spiritual growth. The challenge is to know when dharma talks about consciousness and personal frequency fall on deaf ears when life challenges test comprehension. Many people resort to playing with their delusions, which is why it can take many lifetimes to move up consciousness levels towards enlightened Buddhahood and return to the void once more for infinity. When pushed to the far extreme in any situation, you see what you are made of and what you truly are. That's when master teachers are revealed, and students step down. The energy of the master Buddhist teacher is magnanimous because they are attuned to the core vibration of the Lord's consciousness.

Ultimately, every Buddha will retire from exploring parallel multiverses and return to the spiritual void of non-duality to get reunited with the eternal source energy of the universal one mind, the main Buddha or Lord of all creations in the game. At some point in infinity, you may pop out of the void to explore creation again and then return home once more. This is the eternal gift given to everyone. Everyone creates their reality. *Everyone is a split of the divine, and the divine resides inside every sentient being in creation.* Every woman, every man, every child, and every sentient being in all the cosmos is a split of the divine playing their part to perfection. Cultural hierarchies and classifications do not apply in the higher levels of energy. Everyone is interconnected through the energy of the universal one mind, which resides inside all sentient beings. It is the delusions of humans that place a hierarchy to subvert one another, which appease one's ego. In truth, all sentient beings are a speck of the universal one mind, which is learning and experiencing itself from within its living creation of you.

You can do what many Buddhas of the past, present, and future do, which is to explore multiple parallel realities from within your sacred geometric Merkaba. You may exit the void to play in the game of physicality, non-physicality, in the spirit world, or any other experiences in the cosmos. When you're ready to let go of your identity and your addiction to all of creation, then you're welcome to return to the void of non-duality anytime infinitely. You may even pop out of the infinite void to experience various incarnations as a Bodhisattva in a game that interests you before returning to the void of non-duality once more. Remember to leave each reality a little better than when you entered and always journey well.

Shakyamuni Buddha with Avandana Legends, Wikimedia, Public Domain License

Chapter 1

What is Sacred Geometry?

"Do not follow the ideas of others, but learn to listen to the voice within yourself. Your body and mind will become clear and you will realize the **unity of all things**."

-Dogen, Zen Buddhist Master
Brought Zen Buddhism to Japan.

What is sacred geometry? Well, let me tell you what it is. First, sacred geometry is well documented in Buddhist artwork, as seen in

Buddhist mandalas. However, what has been vaguely understood in the Buddhist tradition is how to interpret the wisdom and science behind Buddhist mandalas. As you read this research book, you will get to know the scientific and medical research that I gathered over the last 20 years to support my lifelong understanding of Buddhist mandalas. The wisdom of all the sages in our historical records and even before our known recordings of ancient civilizations lay hidden in sacred geometry.

    I will break down the parts of sacred geometry and then put them back together so you can see for yourself the meanings behind these symbols. All the wise sages and all the high calibrating wisdom keepers and seekers throughout history come to the same conclusion about our reality. That ultimate truth can be understood by studying sacred geometry. However, even Buddhist monasteries that document sacred geometry in their artwork will tell you that many Buddhists believe this symbol and meaning of sacred geometry in Buddhist mandalas in the retelling of Buddhist oral folklore to go as far back as ancient Lemuria and many ancient civilizations of the past before the megaflood. The knowledge has been preserved through the scribes in free Buddhist universities, which became known as Buddhist monasteries over time.

Sacred geometry is not owned by any spiritual, religious, and academic traditions because it has been rinsed, reused, and even rediscovered throughout the ages in so many traditions worldwide. Even without anyone getting insight into sacred geometry by experiencing a spiritual awakening or Gamma meditation, I believe humanity would eventually stumble on the wisdom of sacred geometry through academic pursuit to study the holographic nature of reality.
According to Wikimedia Foundation, Inc., "Mandala has become a generic term for any diagram, chart or geometric pattern that represents the cosmos

metaphysically or symbolically; a time-microcosm of the universe, though it originally meant to represent wholeness and a model for the organizational structure of life itself—a cosmic diagram that shows us our relation to the infinite, the world that extends beyond and within our minds and bodies" (Wikimedia, 2020). That's the closest definition I have found in academia so far.

However, from my Buddhist understanding, sacred geometry is everything and nothing at all. It is the primary energetic form of all creation. In Buddhism, harmonics are wave particles of sound that can ignite form when played at specific frequencies. In terms of Buddhist mandalas, every mandala represents its unique frequency, representing the ascended teacher's unique attributes in the middle of the mandala artwork. Everything in creation, including people, is made up of energy waves and has a unique sacred geometric mandala shape to its identity. Everyone is working on perfecting their mandala to manifest with ease and live a more expansive and enjoyable life full of love and inner peace.

When I was a child, my family would go to the Buddhist temples in Seattle, WA, USA. I often could not sit still very long, so I wondered throughout the temples we attended. We went to a few different ones. I always wandered off to look at the Buddhist art displayed in the monasteries. I also browsed the artwork in the various books available to people, which many people did not examine as closely as I did. Some monks would explain that mandala artwork is the energetic vessel of different enlightened Buddhas who are using their heightened state of consciousness to travel to different worlds.

I know, that sounds very magical and fantastic! I was told that if I studied the material well enough and became self-aware enough, I will notice the minor, subtle changes in my reality. In reality, those slight changes are your confirmation of how you can move through the empty spaces of time and dimensions, one step closer and closer to the reality you enjoy best. You are the game-changer, and you too can influence the game many people are blindly existing in. Yet, the Lord Buddha is the one mind in everyone playing different roles. Reality benefits from every new person who has raised their consciousness level to a new, more robust energy level because it is one less person who struggles to exist in a lower reality. An awakened Buddha does not change reality. Instead, an awakened Buddha shifts to another reality, leaving a little positive residue that slightly uplifts the last reality they resided in. High-frequency Buddhas' collective consciousness leaves a large residue that imprints various realities and lifts the tides much more.

  The act of raising their level of consciousness shifts the awakened person into a new parallel reality that matches their energy level. All parallel realities already exist. However, moving your perspective on something changes your frequency, and then the environment around you slightly changes to show you shifted into a new parallel reality. *Remember, you never change what's reflected in the pond you are looking at. When you change your perspective, the reflection in the pond mirrors what is inside you.* It's just how energy organizes around more potent power sources. The reason why is because every time a tiny atom becomes expansive and more powerful in its energetic nature, then all energy around it cannot help but grow a little more expansive as well.

A monk told me that I would see the changes if I have the eyes to see. If I have the knowledge to be, then I will be. Now go off, little one, and return to your family to meditate and receive your blessings from the Dakinis. Dakinis are typically female enlightened Buddhas, but they are any person who reaches Buddhahood. As I grew up studying the Buddhist mandala artwork, I loved the folklores around them about how all the male and female Buddhas who reached Buddhahood are flying around from one world to another world. I enjoyed how these enlightened Buddhas manifest their reality and shift to various versions of themselves, like magic, the experiences they desire. I thought these were all Buddhist folklores about gods and goddesses that created their worlds. Little did I know at the time that those Buddhist folklores and teachings are storytime tales of how reality does function.

Once I got into college at the University of Washington, I began to follow the efforts of many Buddhist monks and nuns who volunteered themselves as subjects for mindfulness, consciousness, and metaphysics research in academia. I followed the works of many notable and courageous medical and scientific researchers in academia who studied what they called "pseudo-science." These fringe topics caught my attention because academic universities were having active discussions with the 14th Dalai Lama and many other notable Buddhist lecturers about the nature of reality and consciousness.

The Buddhist mandala artwork I memorized as a child started to become more real as I became more familiar with the flood of knowledge that these research findings were uncovering. Metaphysics in Buddhist mandalas is not folklore or tall tales, but it is really how our reality is designed. Everyone's level of consciousness does factor into its design. This chapter will go over the different scientific research I uncovered that explains what sacred geometry in Buddhist mandalas is.

Everyone is constantly shifting into an existing parallel reality that matches their personal vibration. Sacred geometry is the energy signature that every sentient being in creation is. Everyone is energy. The consciousness within that energetic Merkabah is what decides which parallel reality to experience next. In Buddhism, the challenge is to coexist peacefully with your individual ego so you can experience the most enjoyable ride in the holographic game of physical life. Invite your ego to be part of the greater reality because your narcissistic ego loves to be loved more by the universal one-mind than fighting against the stream for individual glory. Your soul is the consciousness that resides inside you and other people observing the personal growth of the particular aspect of the universal one-mind, Lord Buddha itself.

Sacred Geometry in Earth's Grid

Anthropologists may have found that Earth's planetary grid is an icosahedron by mapping high magnetic field locations in anomaly zones such as the Bermuda Triangle. The icosahedron is the shape of Metatron's Cube, which is also commonly referred to as the sphere of creation. Metatron's Cube is a sacred geometric energy form that includes all other forms in sacred geometry. Popular forms of sacred geometry that can be found in the making of Metatron's Cube are the Flower of Life, Seed of Life, Tree of Life, the Golden Ratio, the Golden Spiral, the Golden Mean, Phi, Fibonacci, tetrahedron, hexahedron, octahedron, and the dodecahedron. These are all platonic solids in math and often seen in creating the popular Flower of Life symbol that we have witnessed reused repeatedly in many religions and spiritual traditions.

These symbols in Metatron's Cube have shown up unbiased in many traditions throughout history from the ancient Tibetan Book of the Dead, Free Masons, Judaism, Hinduism, Mayan, Celtic, ancient Egyptian, and many more ancient lost civilizations that only leave these symbols decorating ancient megalithic temples. The sacred geometric symbols adorned in the ancient temples are so old that we do not know how much older they are compared to our advanced technology of the 21st century. These sacred symbols in sacred geometry can be found in studying Earth grids and higher energy axis points worldwide.

Metatron is believed by many mystic traditions to be an archangel that helps in the creation process. The message mapped out in math as depicted in sacred geometry is an infinite unbreakable truth in nature. Everything exists in unity, harmony, and oneness. Suppose we live in an icosahedron Earth grid as proposed by sacred geometry research. In that case, everything people focus on with their emotions and thoughts will manifest at a faster rate than before we entered the higher vibrating sphere. Planet Earth is the higher vibrating sphere we all travel in. Sacred geometry architect Richard Buckminster Fuller lovingly referred to our planet as Spaceship Earth.

They found in sacred geometry research that when things are built with sacred geometry proportions in mind, then the form is strong. Once the structure's form is strong using sacred geometry proportions, then the energy inside it is high frequency. Low, dense energy cannot exist in an area that is a high frequency. Richard Buckminster Fuller showed this to be true when he created architecture designed after sacred geometry, which many people refer to as "Bucky Balls." Richard Buckminster Fuller studied India's yogis's energy frequency and proposed that a person who has a high level of consciousness radiates at a 5th dimensional level of unity consciousness, much like the five platonic solids of Metatron's Cube.

The Earth grid has all the sacred geometry layers in Metatron's Cube. Therefore, it is leveling up its frequency into a 5th dimensional level of consciousness, which is unified consciousness compared to separatism. Metatron's Cube in Buddhism is a mandala. A strong mandala that Buddhism refers to is an enlightened person who is traveling from one dimension to another in a strong Merkabah. A strong Merkabah is a term used in Judaism for the vessel that an enlightened person is, which in Buddhism, a mandala is made up of sacred geometry. In Buddhism, everyone is energy in an energy orb, which we call our human energy field. That field is made up of sacred geometry. The Merkabah aura field of humans and the Earth's grid's energy field are both designed with sacred geometry.

When a person becomes a unity consciousness in Buddhism, which radiates at a 5th-dimensional unified field of sacred geometry, they often will manifest their fears first to release unconscious conditioning. Once abundance blocks are released, the positive experiences start surfacing to create loving experiences. If someone has been deceiving others and fearful of their secrets surfacing, then such fears will appear so they can be forgiven or transcended through graceful amends. We may live in an era where all truths emerge to start co-creating more beautiful experiences through a unified collective consciousness. This is why it's essential to live a life guided by your higher self than by your ego and live from your heart, training your mind. Some may have a hard time working through their fears in this era of unity consciousness or oneness.

To further understand how sacred geometry is also in Earth's grid system through high energy points in her meridian and understand that even Earth is a conscious being connected to the rest of the living species on Earth, Sir Alfred Watkins discovered ley lines in 1921 (Wikipedia, 2020). He used dowsing rod techniques to map out the magnetic field lines on the Earth. As he was doing his research using dowsing rods to trace where all the high-frequency energy meridians of Earth are, he often found sacred monuments reside along these energy grid paths on the Earth. Once he found a high energy marker in his research, he discovered that the axis points along the sacred pathways often had a large abundance of energy like a vortex.

Whenever he discovered an axis point, he had spiritual experiences. One such spiritual awakening was triggered at an axis point near Stonehenge by his home. Sir Alfred Watkin's work was able to show that the Earth functions like energy lines that follow sacred geometry patterns. Over and over again, the axis points began to create graphic repeat patterns that resembled the Flower of Life axis points and Metatron's Cube axis points. When he put axis points together, it created a sphere with energy grids that move in a "wheel within wheels" design as depicted in many ancient texts and artwork around the world.

The Earth's magnetic ley lines form an icosahedron platonic solid in math. The axis points where the lines intersect are often where large cities are formed. His research following the high energy axis points of the Earth's magnetics leads him to believe that most people are attracted to these magnetic points. It is as if humans, much like animals, are lured in magnetically by a colossal magnet pulsating out energy through these axis points on Earth. The largest magnet on our planet that affects humans' energy is the planet Earth itself (Williams and Hagens, 1984).

Most ancient temples and monuments around the world, such as all the worldwide pyramids, pagodas, and other monolithic structures, reside along the Earth's magnetic ley lines. Sir Watkins discovered many high-energy churches in his country if not all of these iconic structures are built right on top of the Earth's sacred geometric axis points. Many new churches and megaliths are built on top of old holy sites, often on Earth's ley line axis points (Williams and Hagens, 1984).

The Flower of Life is believed to be the first completed life pattern formed out of sonic vibrations from the basic Seed of Life structure. These patterns show up in various religious artworks throughout indigenous mandala artwork, such as seen in ancient Buddhist artwork, ancient

Egyptian artwork, and much older mystic spiritual traditions. The Flower of Life pattern, the Seed of Life pattern, tetrahedron platonic solid, hexahedron platonic solid, octahedron platonic solid, and the dodecahedron platonic solid in math all fit into the 5th element, which is Metatron's icosahedron cube.

If you look further into Metatron's Cube, you will see what many Buddhists have seen for over 2,555 years: the two-dimensional Star of David in Judaism. The Star of David is also the two-dimensional mandala often depicted in Buddhism. When the six-pointed Star of David is depicted in three dimensions, it is all the platonic solids that make up sacred geometry. When all the platonic solids are combined into one structure, it makes up the two-dimensional Sri Yantra in Hinduism. The three-dimensional version of the Sri Yantra makes up the fifth-dimensional icosahedron in sacred geometry, which shows that there are many different ways to see Metatron's Cube. I recognized the different ways that the universal one-mind expresses itself. Through-out history, many Buddhist universities have plenty of educated scribes that document this knowledge about enlightened beings who travel different dimensions in their mandala. The wisdom behind sacred geometry is remembered in plain sight through the Flower of Life decoration in many lost ancient civilizations. Much evidence remains underwater. We know about these ancient lost civilizations that use sacred geometry in their culture through folklores.

As documented in Buddhist artwork in many Asian temples, one of the Buddhist folklores is that this metaphysical symbol of sacred geometry and mandalas goes further back to ancient Lemuria and the ancient civilizations at that time. However, this universal knowledge about sacred geometry has found multiple ways in history to show up, which is separate from ancient sources that may hold this information within the decorations in their lost civilizations.

Even in mathematics, the knowledge of universal oneness through all of creation has been discovered in mathematical formulas of the Phi number, Fibonacci ratio, Golden Ratio, and even the Golden Spiral can be mapped consistently in all sacred geometric forms. Studying sacred geometry shows that we are all interconnected in how we are created through kaleidoscopic proportions. In short, studying sacred geometry tell us that we're all one. We are all energy as mapped by the sacred geometric math to create the sound waves of your spiral coiled DNA. Therefore, as you understand what sacred geometry is, you begin to see that planet Earth is also made up of the same sacred geometric proportions: the people and all sentient beings in creation. All people are connected to the largest magnetic field, which is Earth itself. Whatever frequency she sends out through her axis points will calibrate the animals, including humans living on Earth.

Whenever the Earth changes its energy frequency by sending out higher and higher energy out its axis points, it does affect people. The Earth itself has a consciousness, and it is the biggest magnet. When the biggest magnet shifts its frequency through its axis point, it affects the animals and even the humans living on it. People who are working on raising their consciousness to a 5th-dimensional, unity consciousness frequency to match what energy the Earth sends out will adjust reasonably. All other people of lower frequency struggle to adapt to the conditions of the cosmic storm.

However, people and animals who do not match the sacred geometric energy frequency that the Earth sends out from these sacred geometric energy points will likely adjust their energy frequency negatively. The reason why is because a magnet such as the Earth only amplifies the existing energy. Since people and animals are energy beings, the Earth will amplify whatever positive or negative energy those beings radiate at.

Therefore, if you have repressed abundance blocks or trauma hidden, those traumas will resurface to address, let go of the anger you held about it happening to you, or transform such issues positively. If you do not have abundance blocks to address because you have already addressed them, then what will surface for you is more of what you are: positive opportunities. The higher energy levels cannot hold dense, stuck energy of lower consciousness, which is why old issues are brought up to address and released.

When studying sacred geometry in engineering, researchers Ken Snelson and Jon Monaghan show us in their research that the icosahedron weaving pattern is strong. Their research found that when they weaved fabric in an icosahedron pattern, it first turned fabric into a steel cloth-like texture and then back into a simple cloth. This insight allows new advancements in engineering by developing a new appreciation for sacred geometry. At the University of California at Los Angeles (UCLA), research on sacred geometry discovered that most diseases inspected under a microscope form in a geometric pattern.

UCLA discovered that most viruses are made up of a water component, which forms an icosahedron shape. Through research, academia finds that the Earth is moving from the tetrahedron energy body, which is the exact pattern of the Jewish Star of David and becoming Metatron's crystalline icosahedron grid. As Earth levels up its grid patterns, it will awaken more people into a higher state of unity consciousness. In the continuation of gaining a deeper understanding of what sacred geometry is, sacred geometry researcher Charles Gilchrist explains that the basics of creation in the language of sacred geometry through energy frequencies are also proven correct in cymatics experiments.

The dodecahedron platonic solid can be confused to look much like an icosahedron platonic solid for many math students. The caveat is that the icosahedron platonic solid is transcendental. It can be both a dodecahedron and icosahedron, but the dodecahedron platonic solid can only be itself. The distinction is that the dodecahedron fits inside an icosahedron. However, the icosahedron platonic solid does not fit inside a dodecahedron platonic solid. That is why the icosahedron is a transcendental platonic solid because it can be seen as both the dodecahedron and the icosahedron at the same time. All five platonic solids put together make up Metaton's Cube, which is why it is often viewed as a 5th-dimensional structure. When the Earth connects its axis points to complete Metatron's Cube, it becomes 5th-dimensional in terms of energy.

    Our linear thinking is what throws us off. One has to be one, then the other, but what if it can be both? That's the trick question. That's what throws a lot of people off about sacred geometry. Metatron's Cube is an esoteric, transcendental form that can collapse within itself smaller and smaller and still maintain its form into infinity. Metatron's Cube functions much like a Mandelbrot Set. In contrast, it can also expand larger and larger and hold its shape into infinity. Charles Gilchrist explains that an icosahedron is a transcendental form that looks that way because it has both the dodecahedron and the icosahedron inside it, because the dodecahedron fits inside the icosahedron and not the other way around.

Here's another way to see that sacred geometry is in all creation. Mental health doctor, David R. Hawkins of the Institute of Advanced Spiritual Research, spent his life mapping out the human consciousness to emotion through kinesiology studies. David R. Hawkins is a life member of the American Psychiatric Association and had fifty years of clinical experience. In his lifelong work of measuring an individual's human energy field's energy, he found that different people radiate different colors in their aura field, showing their spiritual, not religious acumen.

Religions function in a separatist belief structure that classifies people. Spirituality is an understanding of cosmology through oneness with the universal one-mind that resides in all creation and the sentient beings that exist in creation. A spiritual approach to life is one of unity consciousness and not separatist in its belief system. The consciousness of unity is connected with all sentient beings, and that oneness resides in the energy of sacred geometry. Dr. Hawkin's lifelong research in kinesiology to measure people's spiritual advancement and concepts through the level of energy they radiate at helps tell the truth from falsehood. This research gives fuel to new medical devices that measure patients' health by mapping their aura field. As modern medicine matures from the publication of this book, modern medicine will eventually lead to energy medicine integration. New kinesiology tools that measure a patient's health through the health of their energy field are leading the way to a more holistic approach to wellness (Veritas Publishing, 2009).

Here's even more research to help understand Metatron's 5th-dimensional cube as seen in the structure of sacred geometry. Consciousness research conducted by the Global Consciousness Project at Princeton University, run by the HeartMath Institute and the Institute of Noetic Sciences, discovered that the human body couldn't lie in kinesiology muscle testing. Research in energy shows that humanity shares one collective consciousness tied to the higher mind's unified field. All human beings are interconnected to each other and through higher universal consciousness. This universal one mind is what many religions and spiritual traditions call God or consciousness.

The Global Consciousness Project was created by the HearthMath Institute and the

Institute for Noetic Sciences to find out if all people are connected to Earth's energy signature. They also wanted to know if Earth itself has a consciousness. These institutions did over 20 years of research to put random number generators at the Earth's axis points in 70 locations worldwide and report the analytics to Princeton University for further study. After 20 years of research, I saw that the Global Consciousness Project successfully showed that the axis points where these random number generators are located make sacred geometric patterns. It also shows that the random number generators, which function much like predicting an earthquake, begin to organize hours before a heartfelt event such as a natural disaster or significant cultural event will happen.

The system predicted Hurricane Katrina, the terrorist attacks at the World Trade Center in New York, the Woman's March, and many other events in the United States. It also predicted heartfelt events in the areas where the random number generators are located in other parts of the world. This research shows us that the Earth has a consciousness and is responding to the magnetic energy surge coming from the people in that area where the random number generators are measuring. It confirms that much like animals who get anxious as a herd when they sense impending natural disasters coming and begin to flee to higher ground. People also send out anxiety hours before an event is going to happen.

Time and time again, event logged after another event logged, the data shows that everyone on planet Earth is connected and sensing each other's anxiety through the energy they send out from their heart. Through their research, the HeartMath Institute discovered that all humans send out an energy surge from their heart up to 5,000 times greater than the energy sent out from their brains. Others feel this heartfelt energy surge. Much like the collective anxiety that animals feel before a natural disaster, people also do the same thing. The energy surge that the Earth sends out from its sacred geometric axis points is what scientists call the Schumann frequency (Roger, 2011). Whenever the Schumann Resonance of Earth spikes into higher frequencies away from her standard 7.83 Hz frequency, she moves into higher levels of consciousness. These heart palpitations in the Earth's Schumann Resonance affect the people and animals that live on Earth. It significantly affects people of lower frequency.

Many research institutions in Consciousness Studies are currently investigating the phenomenon of higher aura fields radiating from a recent influx of higher vibrating young adults and children compared to previous generations in mass. The new era in humanity will not compare riches in the physical world, such as what car you drive, how big your house is, how successful you are, and so on. What a spiritual 5th dimensional level of consciousness measures is what your level of spiritual consciousness calibrates at. Such research shows us that the emotions of acceptance, forgiveness, compassion, and unconditional love are the highest emotions that have far more significant effects on the holographic reality we share. These are the embodiments of the 5th-dimensional Earth, and attuning your frequency to the Earth makes shifting into this higher parallel reality much smoother.

Life is not a race but an eternal learning experience for one's spiritual evolution. We are all going on this ride together collectively and in each and everyone's individual lives. Research into energy medicine and consciousness is uncovering more about the holographic matrix we all share and project experiences individually and collectively.

Sacred geometry research shows that the Earth is an icosahedron shape. The icosahedron is the final and last platonic solid of Metatron's Cube of oneness that encompasses all the other platonic solids within it perfectly as an infinite torus vortex.

A torus vortex is a scientific term for the donut pattern that the human body projects in its aura field. Sacred geometry architect Richard Buckminster Fuller lovingly coined a 5th-dimensional Earth entering a minimum level of enlightenment as "Spaceship Earth."

This is why many indigenous mystic traditions believe that each person creates their reality based on how they feel inside. Each person must decide and go through the self-cleansing themselves and enlighten their consciousness to vibrate at a 5th-dimensional crystalline consciousness. In the west, this unity consciousness is known as "Christ Consciousness." In the east, this unity consciousness is known as "Maitreya Buddhahood." No matter the terms used, this sacred geometric unified consciousness connects each other and connects us all with the universal consciousness of the Lord. The indigenous mystic traditions of the Mayans, Native Americans, Egyptians, Celtic, Buddhists, and many more indigenous tribes believe that more people will awaken to becoming self-aware of how to manifest in harmony with the holographic matrix. They likely will work together in unity consciousness as one collective to pull and transform the 3rd-dimensional reality into a 5th-dimensional reality through a transformation process.

Sacred Space & Ley Lines

Sacred space and ley lines are any space that has been dedicated to a sacred purpose. It is used by many spiritual traditions worldwide to commune with the universal one-mind and the spirit world in the physical dimension. In architecture, a balance of harmonics in synergy with the spirit world is achieved through designing a space or building in the proportions of Archangel Metatron's sacred geometry. In Asia, Feng Shui is a tool used to redesign any space into the harmonics that allow for the easy flow of Chi or Prana energy of the spirit world to help with abundance.

The Free Masons factored in sacred geometry by designing many of their buildings in the Tree of Life form layout. Often, they built an alchemical river flowing under or by the building to help connect to the spirit world. Before the Hindus erect any building type, they construct a square from establishing due East and West. Then they lay out the entire building based on sacred geometric proportions. In Buddhism, the temple of Buddha is often designed in mandalas as a square that leads up to a suggestive pyramid with various sacred geometric cubes of the 3rd-dimensional image of the Flower of Life or Metatron's five-pointed star as commonly known in Judaism as the Star of David. The ancient Egyptians used regular polygons in their construction. Many sacred spaces follow the sacred geometry outlined in Archangel Metatron's proportions, including nature and water.

No matter the culture, sacred geometry is used to design sacred spaces for homes, buildings, and many other architectural forms. Following this strategy invites the spirit world to bless such spaces with grace. Even in the study of architecture, many spiritual traditions have alluded to the interconnectedness of the one unified consciousness of the universe, the Lord. If you want to commune with the spirit world that's available anytime to help you, then try to design your home in sacred space using Metatron's proportions.

To amplify your sacred space's energy that you live in or is a gathering place for spirituality, then use dowsing rods to locate the spot on the property that has axis points where energy from the Earth is pouring out of. Building on top or near these magnetic sacred geometric axis points of the Earth will amplify the connection to the universal one mind and multiple dimensions according to Buddhism's mystic traditions.

Sir Alfred Watkins, the man who in modern times discovered ley lines in 1921 through using dowsing rods mapped out the magnetic field lines on the Earth. He found sacred megalithic monuments often resided along these energy grid paths on Earth. The axis points along the sacred pathways often had a large abundance of energy like a vortex. One prime example of a megalithic monument with a high residue of energy coming out of it in England is Stonehenge. His ley line exploration brought him many spiritual experiences at these axis points near Stonehenge, which was by his home. (Williams and Hagens, 1984).

Sir Watkins' work was able to show that the Earth functions like energy lines that follow sacred geometry patterns. When you put together these magnetic axis points, it depicts a sphere that has energy grids. These energy grids move in a "wheel within wheels" design, as pictured in many ancient texts worldwide. The wheel's movement within the wheel's design functions much like a torus vortex that comes out of the center of the axis point then moves around in intersecting movements like an apple, and then downwards and back through the center. The pattern repeats itself to generate a vortex. This wheel within wheels pattern that is circulating into itself is a demonstration of the Flower of Life in motion.

The video "The Practical Magic of Sacred Space" by Freddy Silva is based on scientific evidence he gathers from the book *Secrets in the Fields*. He does an excellent job explaining how pagan traditions have lasted into the modern age through the Free Masons' architecture. The Free Masons infused their pagan mystical knowledge of ley lines and sacred space in the construction of religious churches throughout Europe, which are in the shape of Archangel Metatron's sacred geometry. The form of the Tree of Life is also used in architecture and design to achieve the harmonics necessary to connect to the spirit world for those to connect to the universal consciousness of oneness. Many indigenous traditions throughout history, such as Buddhists, Hindus, Celtic, Kabbalah, and many others, believe in the oneness of all of life in our holographic reality.

No institution or religious organization owns spirituality. Spirituality cannot be copyrighted or patented. However, no matter how short or long, many pathways lead back to the source energy of the one universal mind. Studying sacred geometry through the activity of marking magnetic axis points on the Earth using dowsing rods is one way to see that everyone in creation is interconnected. The Free Mason's coded such knowledge of Metatron's wisdom about sacred geometry in Gnostic Christianity, which parallels other much more ancient architecture through megalithic structures. For others, understanding the wisdom in sacred geometry resonates with their bodies.

Modern researchers also discovered that when they applied sacred geometry into sacred space using these principles, they too benefited from higher energies circulating in their sacred spaces. In studying the proportions of how the Chartres Cathedral was designed, researcher Boris Jansch discovered that it was built based on sacred geometric proportions. It was also designed with the same ley line principles by being built along a river that goes underneath it and alongside it. Home and Garden TV did an episode on "Feng Shui Style." They showed their audience that the art of Feng Shui furniture arrangement provided some quick tips to redecorate your home into a sacred space that will commune with the spirit world to bring in some good fortune according to the Feng Shui philosophy. A house in harmonics is also believed to have healing properties for our psychology.

Sacred geometry architect John Koch wrote in his article, "Sacred Geometry in Building," that a labyrinth in sacred space helps people meditate and helps achieve calm in their stressed state of being. Geoffrey Simmons, Ph.D. at the University of Calgary, wrote in his research paper, "Sacred Spaces and Sacred Places," that buildings are designed on the principles of sacred geometry, communion with nature, and good harmonics through design creates a space of high frequency for those using the space. His research findings detail the techniques that can be used to achieve these high energetic states through architecture.

The reasons for designing architecture based on the sacred geometry principles are further explored by Dartmouth University in their research paper, "Geometry in Art & Architecture: Polygons, Tilings, & Sacred Geometry." Students and professors studying the mathematics of architecture which uses sacred geometry proportions, found that the harmonics and structure created more calm in the people living in it and created calming soundness that resonates in the space.

When researching how geography factors into architecture constructed based on sacred geometry, Tiffany Whitmire at Sweet Briar College wrote in her research paper, "Sacred Places," that a lot of sacred architecture is built on certain geographical factors which point to high energy locators in space. HolisticHousePlans.com, bio-architect Michael Rice has made a career out of designing residential homes based on sacred geometric proportions and principles found in the history of sacred spaces and ley lines. It is believed that a person living in such a sacred space home could live a more calming and harmonious lifestyle due to the influence of the home, which radiates high frequencies.

Seattle was the 1st modern city designed to build power plants and parks along Earth's magnetic ley lines to create a sacred space similar to the magnetics' in Stonehenge and other ancient sites around the world. The city was built in sync with the harmonics of linking a physical dimension to the spirit world. Using ley lines, follow the natural sacred geometric energy patterns that Prana, Chi, the Holy Ghost, or nature spirits use to move along the ley line pathways. Creating a harmonics space with this natural energy pattern is believed to bring abundance and good blessings from the spirit world. Again, finding these natural sacred geometric points of convergence is often found using dowsing rods or magnetic field detectors.

    Seattle is a good candidate for the ley line project because it was close to the Puget Sound, a water source that passed underneath and alongside the city. Water passing through the sacred space is believed to be alchemical in communication with the spirit world. All sacred spaces built on ley lines have a waterway passing underneath them. The Geo Group created the Seattle Ley-Line Project in 1987, an artwork commissioned and funded by the Seattle Arts Commission, which documents the sacred geometric design. Seattle is the first city in America, possibly the first modern city to have its ley lines located and mapped. Sacred places situated all over the world are generally located over various Earth axis points. These electromagnetic fields of energy emanating from the Earth can improve people's well-being and the Earth.

One of the project's goals was to identify all kinds of Earth energies and work in harmony with the Earth Spirit to improve the flow of these energies through-out the Seattle area. In later years, the Ley-Line Project connected to Portland and San Francisco, which linked up these cities' harmonics along the west coast. These three cities are believed to share similar traits in the population's affinity to oneness with nature and mysticism of the ancient past. The intention was to draw high energy consciousness and abundance to the west coast through the Seattle, Portland, and San Francisco area. This includes pulling high-energy and high-frequency people into the area through Earth's resonance (Pettis, 1998). One can say that high energy consciousness manifested in the physical form are people and things that can process an abundance of information, organize information effectively, and produce an expression of themselves that could help reduce humanity's suffering a little more out of ignorance.

I would speculate that high-energy people of higher consciousness are forward-thinking people working in technology to connect the world and provide a medium to aid solutions that reduce suffering and educate people out of ignorance. Such individuals would love Earth. This is the mission that Richard Buckminster Fuller was focused on in his later years. Richard Buckminster Fuller lectured to the youth about the responsibility to use technology to connect the world, reduce humanity's suffering, encourage peace, and be good stewards of the Earth. Richard Buckminster Fuller was an inspiration for the Geo Group.

The primary purpose of the Ley-Line Project was to:
- Identify and map the major ley lines and ley-line power centers within Seattle using dowsing techniques.
- Design and build a series of environmental artworks used to mark and enhance ley line energy. Some megalithic artwork on these energy axis points is an homage to sacred sites worldwide.

In conjunction with the ley line project to map out Seattle and King County with the harmonics of sacred space to be in sync with the spirit world, which keeps Seattle in tune with Mother Earth, eco-artist, Chuck Pettis developed a 72-acre nature reserve and meditation parkland on Whidbey Island in Washington State. It is designed like Stonehenge with massive megaliths and sacred geometric artwork structures throughout the park. It is a nature hike that has stops to interact with different monuments such as Stonehenge and labyrinths. Along with tributes to other metaphysical monuments worldwide to encourage world peace and harmony, such as the Tibetan Buddhist Stupa with Kwan Yin inside and a roll of meditation wheels. A Native American Medicine Wheel for good health for the world is among many sacred spaces and megaliths built above ley lines at the Earth Sanctuary.

The Earth Sanctuary is a must if you're in Whidbey Island, WA, USA. If you visit the Earth Sanctuary, please wear comfortable clothes and make a park donation for its upkeep. You may even see Chuck there walking a labyrinth. My boyfriend, now husband, saw Chuck Pettis cleaning the parking stalls, and Chuck noticed my 5th-dimensional crystalline consciousness Bucky Ball necklace I wore that day. Mr. Pettis immediately struck a conversation about it and told me great stories about studying under Richard Buckminster Fuller. We instantly became kindred spirits and started talking about consciousness and humanity while walking the nearest labyrinth in the sanctuary. All the while, my boyfriend watched me have deep cosmology conversations about the 5th dimension with another wise man. Chuck is the closest I may get to have a conversation with Richard Buckminster Fuller, the spiritually awakened and metaphysical dome structure architect and engineer. Bucky spent his later years speaking to the youth of the future.

Richard Buckminster Fuller had his spiritual awakening in his thirties after overcoming suicide tendencies due to being overwhelmed by the financial responsibility of supporting a young family. He acquired insight into sacred geometry in an awakening vision quest. Those visions of sacred geometry that Richard Buckminster Fuller had fueled his fascination with Metatron's Cube and designing architecture based on sacred geometry. Richard Buckminster Fuller is famous for his term, "Bucky Balls, " representing an icosahedron sphere. Bucky Fuller spent much of his senior years visiting yogis of India and lectured with Indian yogic, Maharishi to the youth of his time to let go of their parent's paradigm of separation as there is no future there to carry on. Instead, build a new, better society with love for everyone as one unified field here on Space Ship Earth.

Chuck Pettis studied under Richard Buckminster Fuller when he was an adjunct professor and was greatly inspired by his lifetime of metaphysical work. I, too, am inspired by Bucky Fuller 50 years later. Below is a picture of Chuck Pettis and myself. Thank you, Chuck Pettis, for being uniquely you and infusing your love for metaphysics into your work to help raise the consciousness of your reality and raise the consciousness of the greater reality we all share. No one made you and your peers' slice time out of your busy routine to do this work, and there are no rewards at all for completing it and funding much of it yourselves. However, there is nothing but gratitude from the upcoming generations of higher frequency people born into Spaceship Earth.

Coffret Christ at the Cluny Museum
National Museum of the Middle Ages

Vesica Piscis

The Vesica Piscis are portals into new experiences. This form has shown up unbiased throughout time in many indigenous cultures and spiritual traditions through the Flower of Life mandala's intersection. A Vesica Piscis is the eclipsed intersection of two intersecting circles. In many spiritual traditions, when two energy circles intersect, the intersection is a portal that someone can walk through to get to new experiences in an alternate reality. In Buddhism, it is believed that the alternate parallel reality can be traveled through portals, which are created within a person's consciousness.

When you inspect the Vesica Piscis even further by interloping more circles upon more circles, then you get the Flower of Life pattern of multiple intersecting circles. Each intersecting link within every circle is a Vesica Piscis. As in the previous articles on sacred geometry, the Flower of Life is a two-dimensional flat portrayal of the Sri Yantra symbols revered as a sacred shape in Hinduism. The Hindu symbol of that spiritual tradition's sacred geometry is often depicted in a two-dimensional flat mandala design. However, when the two-dimensional flat mandala design is rendered into a three-dimensional, physical version of itself and a light is shined through a Sri Yantra's physical version, a Flower of Life pattern is a reflected shadow of the Sri Yantra on the ground. This effect happens because the intersection points on the Sri Yantra's physical version functions like a Vesica Piscis. This is because a Sri Yantra in three-dimensional models is a physical replica of the Flower of Life pattern.

If you take the intersections between the intersecting points within a Flower of Life symbol that is commonly referred to in many spiritual traditions as the Vesica Piscis and connect them, what is left is the blueprints to make the Hindu Sri Yantra symbol. This image of Jesus inside a Vesica Piscis depicts the awakened person traveling between different realities through their inner portal. The Flower of Life symbols surrounding this image of Jesus in a Vesica Piscis show that the Vesica Piscis is a version within the Flower of Life symbol. The Flower of Life symbol is another version of the Sri Yantra symbol. The Sri Yantra symbol is another version of sacred geometry, which fits into the Metatron's icosahedron platonic solid for how all things in creation are modeled from. The design of Metatron's Cube shows how all things in creation are interconnected and unified. Therefore, nothing is separate from the one universal mind that resides in all of creation.

Let's explore other ways we see the Vesica Piscis being a representation of a portal into new gateways. Your eyes are the shape of a Vesica Piscis. The simple function of the eyes is used to see new experiences through them. Eyes function like a lens to see things with and send those images to your brain to process what you see with your eyes. Again, your eyes are a portal. Here's another example of the Vesica Piscis functioning like a portal to new experiences. A woman's vagina is designed in the shape of a Vesica Piscis. A woman's vagina allows for babies' birth, which is a result of a sexual union between a man and a woman. That sexual union is the physical representation of two people interacting with each other through intercourse. Sexual intercourse is the physical act of a symbolic union. Let me expand on this further.

To understand this, let's take the human aura that radiates around every human being. It has been measured in science that every human being has an energy field around their body, commonly referred to as a human aura. When two people connect, their large circular energy fields are intersecting like circles overlapping each other. This overlapping of circles creates a Vesica Piscis portal. Therefore, when a man and a woman have intercourse, they create a portal between each other, and the possible outcome is another physical representation of these two people. A baby is the outcome of the union between a man and a woman through intercourse. A woman's vagina is the portal that brings forth a new soul into our reality from the spirit world, creating a unique parenthood experience for both people.

The concept of a portal through the Vesica Piscis is also seen in the birth of new universes through the smashing of two stars, creating new galaxies. In science, it is conceptualized that a new universe is created through the intersection of two nebula stars colliding with each other. The Vesica Piscis is a shape that is the intersection of two circles with the same radius, intersecting so that the center of each circle lies on the circumference of the other. When the National Aeronautics and Space Administration captured the collision of two stars with the Hubble telescope, they say that even in science, the intersection of two nebula stars creates a portal Vesica Piscis. This iconic image of space in action shows an image that looks much like an eye pupil inside the Vesica Piscis.

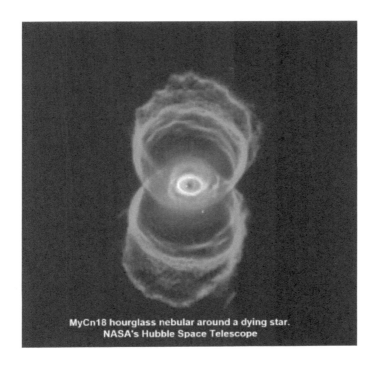

MyCn18 hourglass nebular around a dying star.
NASA's Hubble Space Telescope

The Vesica Piscis pattern of connecting equal circles creates the Flower of Life mandala crops up unbiased in many religious and spiritual traditions worldwide. We get insight into how people are designed through intersecting circles. Professor Charles R. Henry at the Department of Sculpture at Virginia Commonwealth University wrote his findings in "Sacred Geometry: Linking the Human

Form to the Great Pyramids." Charles Henry discovered that when you take two bubbles, merge them in photography and then repeat this pattern, again and again, you make an image of a person. What Charles Henry discovered by intersecting reflective spheres over each other is that the form of a human being is the outcome of continued overlapping circles. He did this exercise digitally.

This is the same as when two cells merged in the mitosis process. The mitosis process of cell division upon each other is how a baby is formed in the womb of a woman's body. When conception occurs through sexual intercourse between a man and a woman, the cells inside the amniotic sac where the baby is grown inside a woman's body until it matures for delivery out of the mother's womb, becomes the shape of spheres that start to merge against each other. These spheres form many Vesica Piscis. This continued merging of new and newer Vesica Piscis in cell division grows to a seemingly infinite level that produces what Charles

R. Henry discovered in his research: sacred geometry develops into a human body when reflected against each other. Take a closer look at this image below the mitosis process in cell division when creating a baby. You can see in the image that each human cell is at various stages of Vesica Piscis. Some cells have one sphere inside them. Other cells have two, three, or four spheres inside them. Some other cells have five or more spheres inside them, which look much like the Tree of Life and the Egg of Life. Once enough spheres are duplicated in the cell, the spheres begin to collide to create many Vesica Piscis like the Flower of Life symbol. When this Flower of Life replication occurs, what transpires is the form of a human fetus, which grows into a baby's body. Professor Charles Henry discovered this exact outcome when he replicated spheres using his computer.

The human experience is believed to exist within a Vesica Piscis, which exists within an even greater interconnectedness in the Flower of Life pattern in Metatron's Cube of oneness. As believed by many spiritual traditions worldwide, the cosmic meaning of the Vesica Piscis is that when two opposing energetic forces come together, they naturally will merge to create new experiences in harmony. This union grows by connecting to more and more Vesica Piscis that complete the Flower of Life, which shows that we are all energy. The Vesica Piscis is a component of sacred geometry. When studying sacred geometry, we see that all things in creation are designed base on sacred geometry. Therefore, we are all part of collective consciousness.

Humanity's progress or self-destruction depends on our ability to realize our connectedness long before we destroy ourselves and the planet, which may not sustain humanity much longer in the 3rd dimension. In Buddhism, it is believed that people who do not respect and acknowledge the oneness of all people as self-reflections lower the vibration of their human aura field. By living in a lower energy frequency by holding separatist beliefs about their interconnectedness to other people and all of creation, they descend to a lower spiritual evolution level.

As a result, in Buddhism and many other mystic traditions worldwide, they believe that these people move to a reality that is of a lower frequency which matches the energy level they radiate at. In contrast, those who work with connectivity radiate at higher resonance, and therefore shift into more abundant parallel realities. Again, there is no right or wrong way to shift between parallel realities. Everyone is on the path that fits their resonance.

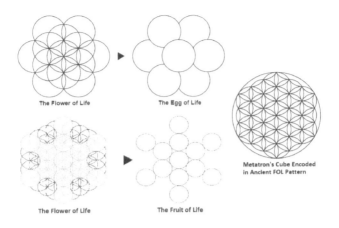

Flower of Life Research Leads to Metatron's Cube

You're probably getting the point about all this research into sacred geometry and how it leads to a personal spiritual awakening within oneself. However, I followed these research papers and sacred geometry findings in many areas of interest for over twenty years. I followed the initial effort of many prominent Buddhist monks and nuns who joined forces with academia to research metaphysics. This is the material I can report on. So the rabbit hole carries on. I am breaking down all aspects of sacred geometry in many religious traditions and then putting it back together to explain the concepts behind Buddhist mandalas.

The Flower of Life mandala artwork isn't a flat image of a flower. When you look at the Flower of Life artwork in many modern religious churches and even on many ancient temples of the ancient past, you begin to see a sophisticated math formula. This sophisticated math formula is coded within a three-dimensional structure of sacred geometry, consisting of 64 points. The Flower of Life symbol is seen in the artwork on the Osirian Temple in Abydos, Egypt, in King Herod's Palace in the 1st century, in the Flower of Life energy ball that the two lions that adorn the gates of the Forbidden City in Beijing, China, in many depictions of Buddha's hand, in the Hampi Indian Temple, in the Library of Celsius in Turkey, and we even see it in the Flower of Life sketches of Freemason member, Leonardo Da Vinci.

The ancient temples around the world that display this beautiful Flower of Life artwork, which many vandals didn't destroy, is the missing link that has waited a very long time for curious people to research further. Although I am familiar with sacred geometry in Buddhist mandalas, I continued to investigate the works of many academic and spiritual visionaries who work together to search for the common truth in all the world's religions, in archaeology, and in anthropology to put the clues together. They intended to understand why this Flower of Life mandala artwork shows up in many temples through-out history.

Well, now we know through awakening into the universal consciousness that for whatever reason destroyed our advanced civilizations of the past, some people left clues in our ancient temples using the Flower of Life symbol. It's believed by many mystics that our ancestors may hope that someday their children will awaken and stop the lower vibrating feuds. Instead, the children of higher frequency will successfully unite as one consciousness for the betterment of each other towards reclaiming our rightful place as worthy self-expression of the universal one's consciousness.

Quantum Physicist Nassim Haramein studied the significance of the Flower of Life symbol. After having a spiritual awakening at 15 years old, Nassim spent his career proving sacred geometry as understood in metaphysic traditions to be accurate understandings regarding universal spirituality's oneness. He explains that these beautiful ancient artworks are codes to activate a sophisticated energy source known in modern math as the Abha Torus Vortex. The Abha Torus Vortex generates continual free energy from a non-local consciousness known as the one consciousness of the Lord.

A vacuum wormhole of unlimited energy, commonly known as a black hole, is created inside the Abha Torus Vortex. Every living being has the potential to activate a wormhole vortex within its body. The instructions are given through an awakened consciousness. In the famous lecture series "Sacred Geometry & Unified Fields" by Nassim Haramein, he provides a complete understanding of the math and lab experiments he performed to show how the unified field was completed out of studying sacred geometry. He began his research by trying to understand the Flower of Life symbol. He noticed that this symbol continues to show up in many ancient temples he studied.

These temples are in different regions of the world, and many of these temples are entirely separate from one another. Yet, the Flower of Life symbol shows up in many ancient temples. From studying the design of the Flower of Life, he was able to render it's intersection points between the circles to see that if you put the Flower of Life symbol into a three-dimensional model of a donut shape and fold over the Vesica Piscis intersections between interloping circles, you get a pattern that looks like two donuts. Nassim then used his understanding of energy flow from his physics profession to explain the vortex function further. He explains that the flow of energy goes from the inside out around the donut shape, down to the bottom, and then back up again. This flow of energy repeats itself over and over again. Nassim calls this donut shape of energy flow, which looks like the Flower of Life in motion the Abha Torus Vortex.

He discovered that this vortex shape is how energy flows in nature. It is also how energy flows around the human brain. An even more giant size vortex of energy flows around the human energy body. The Abha Torus Vortex of energy circulating the human heart, which encompasses the human body, is a person's aura field. Nassim also discovered that the intersection points in a Flower of Life pattern have 64 interconnecting Vesica Piscis points. The 64 intersecting points in the Flower of Life are the same interconnecting points as the Sri Yantra spiritual symbol in the Hindu tradition. Nassim used this knowledge to complete his Unified Field Theory, which understands that everything in creation is interconnected. He furthers his research by developing the Ark technology from this understanding.

The article "R. Buckminster Fuller's Jitterbug: Its Fascination and Some Challenges" by Joe Clinton, Ph.D., discusses how Richard Buckminster Fuller's inspiration for the dome architecture sphere shape that he nicknamed "the jitterbug" came from studying sacred geometry. In my study of Richard Buckminster Fuller's lectures, I found that Richard Buckminster Fuller had his spiritual awakening in his thirties after contemplating suicide. After overcoming his afflictions to suicide, he spent much of his thirties studying metaphysics in eastern beliefs, which put him in contact with the angelic realm through meditation practices. While in meditation, he connected to alternate dimensions through his consciousness which helped him understand Archangel Metatron's Cube. Richard learned that Metatron's Cube is the most potent geometric form in creation because it holds all sacred geometry inside it. Like other students who study sacred geometry through one form or another in academics or spirituality, Richard found that this form is discovered by many ancient eastern philosophies and many other spiritual traditions throughout history.

    Therefore, Richard Buckminster Fuller moved beyond a religious viewpoint about the universe's interconnectivity into a spiritual approach to understanding how everything in creation is interconnected through the sacred geometric form in which it was created. Mr. Fuller came to the same conclusion that many spiritual people draw. We are all incarnated from the consciousness of the universal one-mind. Each of us is having an experience that is fulfilling the intentions we set for ourselves before incarnating. He spent much of his later years lecturing to the youth that there is no one to convert through religions. All there is to do is see how everything is connected and live the best version of you to achieve harmony and peace on "Spaceship Earth." No one's separate from each other. Physicists found that the Flower of Life form is the top view of mandalas by collapsing Bucky Ball's Metatron Cube structures.

Many ancient civilizations believe Archangel Metatron to be the right hand being of universal consciousness in the creation process as seen in mandala artwork in Buddhist traditions, Egyptian artwork, and many more spiritual traditions. It consists of all other shapes such as the Flower of Life, the Seed of Life, Tree of Life, Golden Spiral, Golden Ratio, tetrahedron, hexahedron, octahedron, and the dodecahedron. It all fits into the 5th element, Archangel Metatron's icosahedron cube. Metatron's message expressed in sacred geometry is of harmony and unity in nature fueled by positive sound waves in this holographic matrix that Bucky Fuller calls Spaceship Earth.

To further the findings, many quantum physicists who study metaphysics in sacred geometry help develop the unified field vortex math, which proves that the universal consciousness is inside all living things through mathematics. Vortex math is the calculation of math, which is a diagrammed of numbers that create a circular motion that ends up looking like the Flower of Life symbol. Again the Flower of Life symbol in action becomes the Abha Torus Vortex.

Flower of Life in Language Changes DNA

Many people have heard from various sources, including medical research, that you can affect your health through the thoughts and feelings you hold about yourself. If you think that you are sick, then you likely will become more unwell. If you believe that you will be well and heal from your illness and wounds, then you have a higher chance of recovering. Geneticists discovered that human DNA undergoes an evolutionary jump by activating some junk DNA when sending positive frequencies through positive affirmations in gratitude. All linguistic languages can be mapped from sacred geometry in the Flower of Life form that visually shows that language is vibration. In Buddhism, the language and words that a person chooses to say to themselves have an energy signature, and that energy is a feedback loop that calibrates your health. Therefore, reassuring yourself that you are love itself and lovable does generate a healthy body for your soul to live in.

The Flower of Life is believed by many metaphysical traditions to be the 1st completed energetic life form that the Lord created. The complex sound waves of sacred geometric shapes seen in Metatron's icosahedron cube show up in language by studying phonetic languages in Celtic runes. When someone who studies Celtic runes takes a closer look at the Flower of Life symbol, they can easily see every rune pattern can be traced out of the Flower of Life symbol. Each rune symbol represents a theme and clarity that can help someone in their life which they are working with. Even when I studied the Phoenician alphabet, I found, like many other people who studied it, that the Phoenician alphabet is the root ancestor of the Greek, the Hebrew, the Arabic, and the Latin language. These languages are the four major phoneme-based alphabets. Therefore, it is safe to say that even in studying the basics of linguistics, all languages are sound wave vibrations and adheres to nature's laws. It is designed with sacred geometry in the Flower of Life form. Everything is a sound wave. That sound wave is all things in creation, including you, my love. The words one chooses to say and hear sends a frequency that changes human DNA.

There are 64 codons in DNA. I've found that Ancestry.com has an excellent explanation for understanding this. Ancestry.com explains that "The DNA code is the language of life. It contains the instructions for making a living thing. The DNA code is made up of a simple alphabet consisting of only four 'letters' and 64 three-letter 'words' called codons. It may be hard to believe that most of the wonderful diversity of life is based on a 'language' simpler than English—but it's true. This code isn't made up of letters and words. Instead, the four letters represent four individual molecules called nucleotides: thymine (T), adenine (A), cytosine (C), and guanine (G). The order or sequence of these bases creates a unique genetic code." The waves of emotions cause condones to activate. This number of 64 keeps coming up over and over again when studying sacred geometry.

    The reason why is because there are 64 intersection points in the Flower of Life symbol. In the three-dimensional rendering of the Hindu Sri Yantra symbol, the Flower of Life in physical form, there are 64 Vesica Piscis intersecting nods. Everything in creation is made of the same sacred geometric design, which is connected to everything else in the cosmos.

All sentient beings only activate two primary emotions, fear and love. Fear and love have different sin waves. The Buddhist understanding of fear is that it has a shorter frequency. However, unconditional love has a more extended frequency that activates more genetic patterns in your body through activating more condones. In Buddhism, this concept is played out in a loving person who radiates at a higher level of consciousness which emits more potent energy outwards from inside of them. These people affect the cosmos positively. People who are higher frequency heal not only themselves but those around them through their high-energy presence. The person is not doing any healing. It is the field around them that heals and slightly uplifts others' consciousness due to being present with someone who has a mastery of their dominion.

That's because the universe functions using simple math, as seen in the number line we all learned in grade school. Many people are still trying to figure this out in life. This simple understanding is realized in this formula, (+) + (-) = stability, nothing forward & nothing backwards. That's why when you say or do a positive thing and then replace it with a negative, you get in an emotional quagmire. The formula (-) + (-) = -, means that two negatives always go into further descent. When you say or do something negative to yourself and follow with more negativity, you fall into more abyss. When aligned with being positive about an outcome such as this formula, (+) + (+) = +, this means only two positives will amplify and grow as it feeds off each other in unison. This is seen when you do or say something positive to yourself. You feel good, and it is ongoing. Here's the kicker, your brain can't tell the difference if you say or do something negative to yourself or others as your brain sees you, two people, as one being.

Therefore, when you say or do something negative to others, your body still feels the effects of stress, anxiety, and paranoia as if you did it to yourself.

According to Buddhists and many mystic traditions, a continuation of such negativity starts to create stress and ailments in your body. Living in unconditional love for yourself and others activates the Kundalini source energy within your pineal gland as displayed in various 6th senses. This is shown in various spiritual artworks throughout the ages. The funnel torus that looks like a magnetic apple field around your heart is multiple tori insulated within more of itself. It is spinning in a circular pattern up to the top, around to the bottom, and back up again like a black hole.

This mystic description is much like a Russian doll that has smaller versions of itself inside it. In science, this is called a torus field around a person. In an earlier article about the Flower of Life, I explained sacred geometry in the design of all living beings in creation that look like a torus vortex. In many ancient mystic traditions, this is called your "Merkaba." Merkaba can be understood by breaking down the word as "Mer" means Light, "Ka" means spirit, and "Ba" means body. In essence, your Merkaba is the light of your spirit around your body. In yoga, this torus field in science is also recognized as your "aura."

The flow of energy up your body in yoga is your seven chakras, which fuel your Merkaba. The intention of what you feel and think about yourself is the language that you tell your chakras to follow through with. Your chakras then send the energy out into your Merkaba field. Wallace G. Heath, Ph.D., wrote in his published research paper, "Some Biophysical Basis for the Human Energy System," that the human body is made of energy. His research found that the human body produces its energy and radiates out to the world the energy level that a person generates. In his study, he discovered that every living thing is composed of an energy body. That energy field inside and around a living being is an energy field. The health of that energy field that someone radiates at signifies how healthy a person is.

Through their research, the HeartMath Institute found that a healthy and balanced torus field around a person can positively affect themselves and the people around them. Global coherence is an initiative that the HearthMath Institute is working on to help people live heart-centered lives. By doing so, they lovingly affect those around them by being a natural beacon of heart energy. The HearthMath Institute reports that the heart is 5,000 times stronger than the energy sent out from the brain to the people nearby. This difference in energy can be seen in Buddhist mandalas which always depicts an energetic halo around the brain and an even larger aura field around the body of an ascended master teacher of wisdom.

When two nearby people's heart energy radiates out a circular torus vortex (apple-shape) aura field out from their hearts and interconnects between each other, that is what the HeartMath Institute calls "coherence." The HeartMath Institute is working to help achieve global coherence. Global coherence is achieved when many people make a heart-to-heart connection and carry that on to the next person. Eventually, the whole world connects on a heart-to-heart level, and global coherence is achieved. If you are reading this and imagining a picture of what two torus vortex fields sent out from two people's hearts would look like, you will see a Vesica Piscis. As previously discussed, a Vesica Piscis is the intersecting nods or points in a Flower of Life symbol. When the whole world has a heart-to-heart connection, then what happens is a worldwide Flower of Life pattern emerges in humanity's collective consciousness. As explained in the previous article about the Flower of Life as Metatron's Cube, you then have a living matrix of a pulsating Flower of Life energy body around the

Earth. Radiating at a higher frequency energy body of unity consciousness is believed by many mystics to draw humanity into an Earthly dimension that also radiates at a 5th-dimensional collective consciousness.

A lot more on how language affects human DNA is discovered in Dr. Pjotr Garajajev and Vladimir Poponin's research. They published research papers that show that the ancient esoteric knowledge from indigenous traditions taught in Buddhism, Native American, Aboriginal, and many more were mystic traditions are correct. Indeed, positive affirmations at specific frequencies in language expressed in chanting rituals and music change our DNA. Humans can become healthier and happier by awakening to the path of enlightenment through letting go of fear and lousy self-talk, which stunts positive growth. It creates disharmony in the body. Choosing to talk to oneself in an unconditionally loving, compassionate, and forgiving nature does help human DNA stay healthy longer.

Dr. Pjotr Garajajev and Vladimir Poponin made many enlightening discoveries in sound and light frequencies. The two that stick out the most were when they were able to program sound frequencies using words. What they did was say positive words and affirmations to a light ray, and then they shined that light ray with the programmed affirmation and chants to the test subject. The result was that the client suffering from an illness healed faster from their symptoms. They also intercepted the light language spoken through ultraviolet light between two frog embryos in the lab. They took the light language discussed between the two frog embryos and shined it on a salamander embryo. What resulted was a salamander egg developing into a frog. Therefore, the research of Dr. Pjotr Garajajev and Vladimir Poponin shows us that the words that people say to themselves are either making them sick or stay healthy. They also found that words have frequencies, which can be transmitted into the light. The light itself becomes a language that can program DNA.

In the research done by Professor Fritz-Albert Popp of the International Union of Medical and Applied Bio-electrography, he discovered that all living beings' DNA responds to light frequencies. He spent his life studying how specific frequencies emitted through light photons positively affect dying and diseased cells. Dr. Pjotr Garajajev and Vladimir Poponin completed research on how people's words to talk to DNA have different frequencies. When using a particular language to speak to DNA, Dr. Pjotr Garajajev and Vladimir Poponin found that language sets a specific frequency and can be programmed into photon ultraviolet light. When light and sounds frequencies with the new language are programmed into the photon light, it can be played on living beings. This changes their DNA through language.

Now, I repeat this significant scientific finding as a baseline for what Dr. Fritz-Albert Popp discovered about photon therapy. Dr. Fritz-Albert Popp studied the works of Dr. Pjotr Garajajev and Vladimir Poponin. He used the frequencies that they found from programming language into light frequencies, which they applied to cancer patients. Dr. Fritz-Albert Popp discovered that cancer patients had scrambled photon light inside their bodies. His research found that everyone has subtle light flowing inside their cells, and the cells are communicating through the light frequencies. That is why under ultraviolet x-rays, the light particles illuminate when looking at leaves under an x-ray. In short, he found that cancer patients were losing light because there was not an equal flow of light through their cells. Simultaneously, the opposite occurred in muscular sclerosis patients who had too much light flowing through their DNA. In developing photon therapy for DNA regeneration and equilibrium, Dr. Fritz-Albert Popp helps develop medical equipment to use specific light frequencies, which aid the self-regenerative healing properties of impaired DNA.

As the world becomes more interconnected through the internet, we need to remember to be good to ourselves and other living things. This will help maintain a healthy Merkabah aura around our bodies. Suppose people forget to release the restrictions that they may unconsciously place on the energy field around them due to negative self-reflection. In that case, they can find the clues to change their DNA into a healthier state of existence through studying the remnant visual artwork in ancient phonetic languages. These ancient phonetic languages may fit in the Flower of Life pattern. Everyone on Earth and in all creation is interconnected like the Flower of Life in Metatron's Cube. Due to the engineered nature of reality being a feedback loop to how we see ourselves and each other, we cannot only help ourselves be healthier, but we can also help others be healthier by saying positive self-talk.

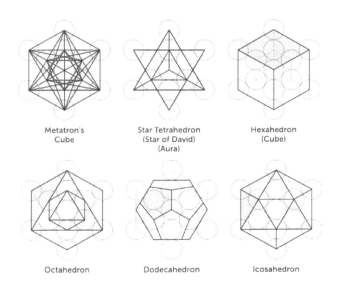

Metatron's Cube

We do not exactly know a lot about Archangel Metatron. There are many accounts for Metatron showing up through-out religious literature in the middle-east. In many versions of religious artwork surrounding Metatron, he is associated with sacred geometry symbols. Sacred geometry is the repeat interloping of concentric circles that form the two-dimensional Flower of Life symbol. However, this understanding of how all creations are based on the sacred geometry design continues to show up in many spiritual and ancient temples worldwide, going much further back beyond the creations of the middle-east's Abrahamic religions. Metatron did not create sacred geometry, but it was rediscovered in the middle-east by Metatron. Metatron's spiritual visions about sacred geometry from his master teachers of consciousness are what Metatron is associated with. Therefore, sacred geometry is commonly associated with Metatron's Cube.

According to Wikipedia, *"Metatron is an angel in Judeo-Islamic mythology, mentioned in a few brief passages in the Aggadah and mystical Kabbalistic texts within the rabbinic literature. Metatron is not mentioned in the Torah and how the name originated is a matter of debate. In Islamic tradition, he is also known as Mitatrush, the angel of the veil.* In folkloristic tradition, he is the highest of the angels and serves as the celestial scribe or [recording angel]. In Jewish Apocrypha and early kabbalah, *"Metatron" is the name Enoch received after his transformation into an angel. Furthermore, the Merkabah text Re' uyot Yehezkel identifies the Ancient of Days from the Book of Daniel as Metatron.*" Regardless of religious canon debate among various sources for Metatron's lifetime, sacred geometry is associated with Metatron as Metatron's Cube. This is due to the depictions of his multiple accounts of communication with heaven through sacred geometry symbols.

Metatron uses sacred geometry to teach about the veil. The veil is the holographic nature of reality. The spiritual teachers from heaven pierced Metatron into his spiritual awakening by lifting the veil to see that reality is a reflection of his level of energy. Conscious insight was realized in his understanding of parallel realities. Metatron taught about consciousness and how changing perspectives changes your frequency. One's level of consciousness navigates their Merkabah to a new parallel reality that matches them.

Islamic portrayal of Metatron in the Daqa'iq al-Haqa'iq by Nasir ad-Din Rammal in the 14th century CE.

When studying Metatron's Cube, one can see that all platonic solids in math fit inside it exactly. The Seed of Life, the Tree of Life, and the

Vesica Piscis are aspects of the two-dimensional viewpoint of Metatron's Cube in the Flower of Life symbol. As seen in the Flower of Life, Metatron's Cube is seen in the artwork of religious text from many Abrahamic religions. The Flower of Life symbol also shows up in many other ancient temples outside of the Jewish, Islamic, and Christian texts.

The Jewish, Islamic, and Christian religions share the wisdom of sacred geometry in Metatron's Cube. All Abrahamic religions share Metatron's accounts in their cannon. Archangel Metatron is the only known archangel that incarnated as a human on Earth. Therefore, Metatron understands from his first-hand experience as a human being what level of suffering and ignorance that the veil has over people. The below image shows that many ancient temples in different places throughout the world also revers the Flower of Life symbol. As archaeology is finding more ancient temples much older than these, they see similar symbols such as the Flower of Life or temples with two lion guards that hold the Flower of Life ball beneath their paws.

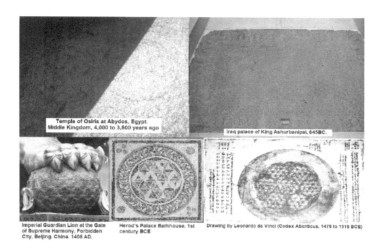

In Hinduism's ancient Vedas text, the Sri Yantra symbol is revered as a sacred understanding of the cosmos through studying that symbol. According to Wikipedia, "The *Samhitas* are the earliest Vedas texts and date roughly from 1500 BCE to 1000 BCE. In the Map of Consciousness work that Dr. David R. Hawkins does, he calibrated the Vedic text as almost 7,000 years old. Therefore, regardless of the original date, the Sanskrit Vedas of ancient Hinduism is far older than many modern Abrahamic religions and spiritual traditions such as Buddhism, which currently is practiced by many people on Earth.

The reason why the Sri Yantra sacred geometric symbol from the ancient Vedic spiritual texts is important is that when you study the intersection points of the Sri Yantra and model its exact proportions into a 3rd-dimensional physical structure, the shadow reflection that comes out of the three-dimensional Sri Yantra is the Flower of Life symbol. Therefore, Metatron's Cube is one symbol in the literature that we have a disjointed record of. The knowledge about enlightenment through studying sacred geometry is also seen in the Hindu tradition in their ancient Sanskrit Vedic text, which is depicted in the Sri Yantra symbol.

Metatron's Cube shows up in many religions as sacred images known as the Star of

David in Judaism. The Star of David is also referred to as the Shield of David, which is a protective talisman in its origins. It is commonly used by Jewish faithful as an identifier of Judaism. In Judaism, their version of sacred geometry is the hexagon shape of an intersection of equilateral triangles. In Hinduism and Buddhism, many ancient mandala designs also use a hexagon from sacred geometry. An awakened, enlightened being always traveled inside the hexagon star. The hexagon shape is a standard sacred image used in many religions and spiritual traditions.

Physicist Nassim Haramein, Ph.D., spent his life working to prove that everyone on planet Earth is interconnected and has access to infinite knowledge with the universal one mind. He was able to confirm this theory of the Unified Field through studying sacred geometry. From studying sacred geometry through many religious and spiritual traditions, in science and math, Nassim came to the same understanding about Metatron's

Cube. That understanding is that there are 64 points in the Flower of Life, which is the same as 64 points in the Sri Yantra. The same knowledge is also in many other forms of sacred geometry.

Nassim refers to this knowledge as the 64 tetrahedral. He uncovered that harnessing the power within Metatron's Cube can harness a black hole of unlimited energy. He also recovered the ancient knowledge that the pyramids' structure is designed off of the proportions in sacred geometry. He believes that the proportions of the pyramids can generate energy. By studying the mystery of sacred geometry, which esoteric believers commonly know as Metatron's Cube, Nassim found that Metatron's Cube creates a connection to the universe's universal one-mind. His life works so far is to educate people on the unlimited technological opportunities that come from understanding sacred geometry because it is the blueprint for anything in creation.

Nassim's Unified Field Theory is put into practice by creating technology based on the 64 tetrahedrons in sacred geometry. New consciousness technology such as the Advanced Resonance Kinetics (ARK), which is made up of 64 amplifying crystals designed after the Sri Yantra in Metatron's Cube, is a leap forward into consciousness technology. Nassim and many others who awakened to the wisdom of sacred geometry work to better-unified humanity.

Even more proof of Metatron's Cube as a design for all of the creations and the unification of interconnectedness in all creations is found through the mathematical formulas of Phi, Fibonacci, Golden Ratio, and the Golden Spiral. These mathematical proportions can be mapped in all sacred geometric forms. Artist Charles Gilchrist explains in his video series, "Sacred Geometry: Pi - Phi - Fibonacci Sequence," that when you draw out the Golden Mean using the spirals of sacred geometry, you can measure the exact proportions of Pi, Phi, and the Fibonacci sequence. Therefore, even using math to understand ratios and mathematical relationships to different areas of space, you will stumble into understanding sacred geometry in Metatron's Cube. The science and technology publication New Scientist published a YouTube video, "What Pi Sounds Like." This was one of the 1st videos that show that Pi's numerical sequence in math is a series of musical notes that play a melody. Sacred geometry equates to mathematical formulas to understand the self and the universe. The math of sacred geometry equates to music songs, which also translates to sacred symbols. The universal one mind is so creative in its multiple expressions of self. Go figure! Phi is a song.

In 1960, Kenneth Snelson stumbled on the proportions of sacred geometry in Metatron's Cube. He documented what he stumbled on in his YouTube video, "Tensegrity to Weaving Transformation," where he weaved a woven cloth in various proportions of sacred geometry. He quotes, "In 1960, while trying to develop an extendable planar structure, I discovered a tension and compression form similar to woven fabric. It is composed of struts that follow a zigzag course; the rigid parts are held firmly in place by tension wires. This animation shows the transformation of the woven cloth into a steel structure and back again".

Kenneth Snelson goes further to explain the intricate weaving patterns he tested out, which are the proportions of sacred geometry in his publication, "Tensegrity, Weaving, & the Binary World." As I examined the weaving patterns that Mr. Snelson documents in his article, I see that he weaved many various platonic solids and Flower of Life patterns in his fabric weaves. He stumbled on a profound discovery, even in weaving fabrics using sacred geometry; the fabric changed its alchemical components into a solid steel-like cosmology in its core and then transformed back to its fabric weave to look like many other fabrics.

Even in medicine, when studying the structure of diseases, many universities worldwide also found that diseases are designed in the shape of an icosahedron platonic solid. An icosahedron is the 5th structure in the formation of platonic solids. I covered this in previous articles, but here is a review of platonic solids. The tetrahedron, octahedron, cube, and dodecahedron all fit inside the proportions of the icosahedron shape. When looking at the icosahedron platonic solid in math, you see that when all the forms are fit into this shape, there are six points on the outer edge. The six-pointed star edges of an icosahedron are commonly referred to in Judaism as the six-pointed Star of David. The icosahedron structure is a 5th-dimensional shape. This is due to it being a composition of all five-dimensional shapes, which fit inside it. The Star of David is another version of Metatron's 5th-dimensional cube of unity consciousness.

The icosahedron unifies all the mathematical proportions. This unification of all the proportions in Metatron's Cube is referred as unity consciousness. In Buddhism and many other mystic traditions, this icosahedron structure in consciousness is revered as the crystalline consciousness. A 5th-dimensional consciousness that resonates at sacred geometric proportions is crystalline in nature. It is crystalline because of the fractal, crystal nature of this energetic shape. Another common translation of crystalline consciousness is "Christ consciousness." Anyone can be Christ-like by radiating at a crystalline level of energy. Christ is a nickname for someone of that level of energy. In Buddhism, the crystalline consciousness is referred to as Maitreya Buddhahood. Maitreya Buddhahood will be discussed further in this book to explain how it is the Buddhist reference to a unification consciousness.

Many highly evolved spiritual master teachers that travel parallel realities in their mandalas radiate at a crystalline consciousness. That is why there are many teachers of consciousness from the Buddhist mystic traditions. All evolved teachers teach at all levels of consciousness to help reduce people's suffering in that parallel reality further out of ignorance before they move onto another parallel reality. It is hard for many higher vibrating teachers of consciousness to stay at low levels too long because their energy is not that dense. Therefore, they will jump into a parallel reality that is more of an energy match to them. *When the student is ready, the teacher appears.* Take good notes of the wisdom because that knowledge will be used to save you from your ignorance, which moves you into lower parallel realities.

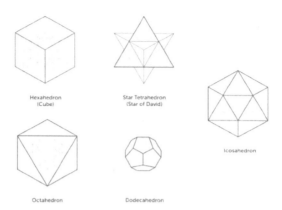

From studying the microscopic structure of diseases, the medical profession found that diseases are designed in a 5th-dimensional platonic solid design, which we know in math as the icosahedron. As explained earlier, Metatron's Cube is a 5th-dimensional structure that holds five dimensions by having all five platonic solids fit inside it. Therefore, this structure functions as a unified consciousness to achieve its intended purposes. The icosahedron can act as a hive mind in connection to the universal one-mind of the universe. This design of the viral icosahedron is discussed further through the Department of

Chemistry, the Department of Biochemistry, the Department of Physics, and the Department of Astronomy at the University of California in Los Angeles, CA completed.

In the research publication of the Proceedings of the National Academy of Sciences of the United States of America, the researchers found that "With few exceptions, the shells (capsids) of sphere-like viruses have the symmetry of an icosahedron and are composed of coat proteins (subunits) assembled in special motifs, the T-number structures. Although the synthesis of artificial protein cages is a rapidly developing area of materials science, the design criteria for self-assembled shells that can reproduce the remarkable properties of viral capsids are only beginning to be understood."

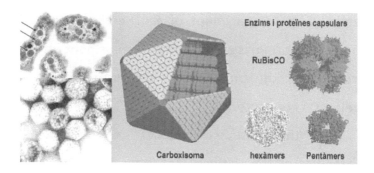

Archangel Metatron's Cube is the most potent geometric form in creation. It holds all other sacred geometry as explained unbiased in many ancient eastern philosophies and other traditions throughout the ages. The message mapped out in the form of conclusive math as depicted in sacred geometry is an infinite unbreakable truth in nature, which is that everything exists in unity, harmony, and oneness.

The icosahedron is documented in ancient indigenous mandala artworks for thousands of years. Metatron's Cube is seen as the basic framework in Buddhist mandalas, with the mandala's center area being an enlightened person. This same basic structure is also found in the symbolic artworks of many other religious traditions such as Hindu mandalas, Jewish star, and many other traditions where these universal symbols are used. The strongest icosahedron shape in the universe consists of all different shapes such as the tetrahedron, hexahedron, octahedron, and dodecahedron. The Flower of Life, Tree of Life, the Seed of Life, Phi, Fibonacci numbers, the Golden Spiral, and the Golden Ratio are found in the icosahedron. Many discoveries coming out of Quantum Physics stem from understanding Archangel Metatron's Cube's sacred geometric shape.

Otherwise, known as the Sphere of Creation in some Abrahamic religious text, Metatron's Cube, which all forms manifest within, continues to educate students studying sacred geometry to learn more about how everything in the cosmos is created. The more we prove mathematically accurate and use such findings of Metatron's Cube to develop new technology, the more we substantiate that the ancient indigenous traditions in many ancient spiritual cultures are correct. Everything in creation is built off the unified conscious design of Metatron's Cube.

Yet, due to colonization, religious imperialism, destroyed records, and lost knowledge through natural disasters in ancient times, the last remaining artifacts that science has derived esoteric knowledge can be found in Buddhist schools of learning and remnant ancient mandala artwork. Many ancient oral traditions and teachings can also be studied in forgotten ancient temples. This knowledge makes it critical for us to forgive ourselves for hurting each other out of ignorance because all religious and spiritual traditions point to the same fact. That fact is that we are all designed from Metatron's Cube, and we are all connected to the universal one-mind.

The scholarly resources discussed provides more information about how advancements in math and science are coming from exploring ancient understandings in remaining documents about the sacred geometry of metaphysical sciences found in Buddhism, Hinduism, Judaism, ancient Egyptian, and so many more historical references to sacred geometry, which hasn't been wiped out due to religious imperialism and colonization. Lost metaphysical knowledge has found renewed interest in modern times through quantum science. In doing so, we are unifying our understanding of all world religions that had fragmented understandings or lost knowledge about sacred geometry. There is no one to convert. We are all sacred geometry existing in a parallel reality that matches our frequency. Some people know this truth. Other people fly blindly through the cosmos.

This rediscovered metaphysical knowledge continues to show up in mandala artwork in ancient civilizations worldwide as we uncover more ancient archaeology. So much blood and pain are shed out of religious ignorance. One important lesson we can derive from studying sacred geometry in Metatron's Cube is that everyone is interconnected to each other and the universal one-mind. The children of planet Earth can choose to reject conditioning from previous generations. They need not continue such madness of seeing everyone as separate from one another. It's time to unify, forgive each other and ourselves, and move forward peacefully.

Chapter 2

Sacred Geometry in Spirituality

"The Buddha is your real body, your original mind. This mind has no form or characteristics, no cause or effect, no tendons or bones. It's like space. You can't hold it. It's not the mind of materialists or nihilists. If you don't see your own miraculously aware nature, you'll never find a Buddha, even if you break your body into atoms."

−Bodhidharma. Started Zen branch of Mahayana Buddhism in China, founded Kung Fu at the Shaolin Temple, and Princess Kwan Yin ascended to Buddhahood from Bodhidharma's teachings.

Many modern religions and spiritual traditions worldwide use the same sacred geometry symbols in their belief systems. The spiritual knowledge about the oneness of all creation and the direct connection to the universal one mind, which resides inside every living being in all of creation equally, has been discovered by mystics from all walks of life and in all parts of the world independent of each other. Anyone in history studying the nature of reality through studying patterns in math, science, biology, music, art, and so many different fields eventually comes to the same conclusions. The conclusion is that there are genuinely no religions in history that own spirituality. Spirituality cannot be owned or branded. Spirituality is the nature of reality, and the truth of reality can only be experienced.

This chapter will go over how various spiritual and religious belief systems have held in their understanding of sacred geometry. These spiritual insights into the nature of sacred geometry are often transferred to the mystic from these different cultures through meditation, which is achieved through various means. As I explain further the meanings behind these long-beloved symbols about enlightenment and a direct connection to divinity, you will see that all religions through-out recorded human history are speaking about the same truths regarding nature and divinity.

The nature of reality and connection to divinity and all things in creation is retold repeatedly through an unbiased formula in sacred geometry. To level up your consciousness to higher peaks, one must understand *that there is no one to convert*. In reality, all that is needed is to be the best version of yourself you can achieve and leave the world a little better off once you return to the non-physical spirit world.

In various cultures, understanding oneself through understanding sacred geometry is often discovered through the flow of how energy moves. Once the movement of energy is observed, the mystic usually begins to see a pattern that forms the Flower of Life in Metatron's Cube. Even the modern understanding of the Flower of Life shows a more in-depth knowledge of how the flow of energy moves, but the pattern remains the same Flower of Life symbol. Even if different mystics in any culture or time in history never saw these symbols through meditation, studying how energy moves and is repeated in nature will eventually be rediscovered.

    I studied mandala artwork in Buddhism since my childhood days, running around the Buddhist monasteries my family participates in. I also studied beautiful artwork of mandalas in Hindu art, which is also incorporated in Buddhist art history. This repeat of imagery in Buddhism is because Buddhism is a branch off of Hinduism's Vedic texts from ancient times. Regardless of the complete picture of fragmented sacred geometry in many spiritual traditions, it all gets put together into a completed mandala artwork that you can find in a mandala.

I continue to focus on putting this enormous piece of the puzzle from all these different religious and spiritual depictions of sacred geometry into mandalas, which is often found in Buddhism, because I learned about sacred geometry through studying Buddhist mandalas. Once I learned about the completed picture and truth behind the meanings in a Buddhist and Hindu mandala, I understood the fractal pieces of sacred geometry in other religions and mystic traditions.

My research puts all the fragmented pieces of sacred geometry from all religions together. This research tells humanity's story of how our fragmented civilizations tried to explain our holographic nature of parallel realities through sacred geometry. In the near present, religions will be an aspect of your spiritual journey, just as DNA is a code for where your ancestors migrated from to get to become what you are today. However, religious heritage does not define who you are or what you become. You, yourself, wield your destiny in your Merkabah. Becoming a conscious creator within your Merkabah dictates the trajectory of which parallel reality you experience next.

Suppose you have not seen the connection of all these various forms of sacred geometry repeatedly replayed throughout the world, then by the time you finish this book. In that case, you, too, will see the meaning behind sacred geometry as blatantly obvious. You also will wonder why you never saw it before. It was staring you right in the eye with how clear as day the meaning behind sacred geometry in spirituality is. Sacred symbols convey the unity of all things as varying expressions of the one universal mind of the cosmos.

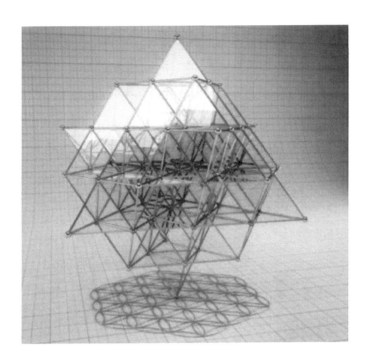

Sri Yantra

The ancient Sri Yantra spiritual symbol depicted in Hindu and Buddhist mandalas is a tetrahedral three-dimensional structure. When the typical two-dimensional drawing seen in many Hindu and Buddhist mandalas is made into a three-dimensional physical structure, the shadow that it reflects shows a Flower of Life design on the ground. This is because the intersection points in a three-dimensional Sri Yantra are the same intersection points in the Flower of Life. When further studying the Flower of Life symbol, it also has the Tree of Life symbol inside it, representing the human chakra system. In many artistic depictions of the Sri Yantra in Vedic texts and Hindu temples, which inspired Buddhism, the human energy chakras are often presented. This is because Sri Yantra is another representation of the proportions of sacred geometry in physical form.

When a student of sacred geometry studies the human aura field and how the Kundalini's energy flows around the body and a smaller aura field flows around the brain. The Flower of Life pattern rotates up the human chakras, then out around the body, and moves back up through the chakras. This flow of Kundalini spiritual energy makes up the human aura, or in Buddhism, they call it the "rainbow body," which is what Hinduism is depicting in the Sri Yantra symbol.

Inside the Sri Yantra tetrahedral structure is the six-pointed Star of David which is often depicted in Judaism, Kabbalah, and Buddhism. In Buddhism, learning to understand and work with our heart and mind is key to tap into universal consciousness and its knowledge. By being a self-aware, awakened person manifesting within our reality, we give ourselves the ability to shift to a reality that is more in line with what our energy field is radiating at. In Kabbalah, that tradition calls this aura energy field your Merkabah.

Your Merkabah is the intersection of two equilateral triangles, which makes up the Star of David symbol. In Judaism and Kabbalah traditions, your Merkabah acts as the shield that protects you. In Hinduism, your Merkabah or Sri Yantra is the energetic vessel that an awakened person travels through different parallel realities in. This is why in many depictions of various Hindu deities and

Buddhist deities, these awakened gods and goddesses often travel through the cosmos in a Sri Yanta or sacred geometric star in mandala art.

From my understanding of studying the Sri Yantra symbol, it is another version of sacred geometry. What keeps people from being self-aware of how to use their Merkabalistic creation powers in this hologram is the lack of insight into how polarity is played. By harboring lower emotions in one's consciousness, such as fear constructs, they will manifest a reality in which the user experiences more of the fearful energy they emit into reality. *Reality is only mirrored to allow the creator of their own experience the ability to see the polar opposite of their thoughts and emotions. Reality is a mirror of what is inside.*

This helps them to decide what resonates within them. Then the universe reads a person's energy signature radiating from their energy body to manifest the next set of synchronistic events to project back to them to be experienced. You are always living from within your heart where the black hole of your Merkabah lies is always to choose the most loving options, so more unified and positive experiences manifest with synchronicity.

Synchronicity is when events with no direct connection seem to fall into place as if by cosmic design. In Buddhism, your soul and spirit group work to align things on your path to help you out. The more of a conscious creator you are, the more synchronicity is a normal part of your life. This book you are reading is a product of synchronicity. Each research was presented to me in seemingly random articles and journals in the library, in random radio ads. One-by-one, each piece of evidence was built on top of one another until a complete picture was understood. It was not a download. It was work. My challenge was to organize it and explain it simply for a novice who is new to sacred geometry.

When your chakras' rainbow body is activated, then black hole energy emits out of your heart chakra. This is depicted as auratic Metta circles around the body. The brain also emits a halo of energy accessed from within someone's consciousness, spinning in a Golden Spiral. It propels you into your desired parallel reality and dimension. Living with an active Sri Yantra through being an awakened person and working on leveling up your consciousness level, you activate dormant 6th senses. Your 6th senses are unique to your DNA, which matches the frequency you previously emitted out into the universe back to you, the creator. They are reflected projections to be experienced in a series of now moments.

In science, they call this process the movement of a black hole where the non-local conscious energy comes down the crown chakra, through all the chakras downward, and then outward in an apple-shaped circular motion back to the crown chakra, and downward in a loop cycle. That's why all black holes follow the same vortex shape of the human aura system around the body.

The halo above the crown chakra, often accompanying the circular apple-shaped torus vortex around the body, represents universal energy starting at the crown chakra and coming down the Tree of Life inside you. That's why all accurate spiritual artwork has a circular human aura and a halo. This flow of energy depicted through the 64 intersection points in the Sri Yantra also represents the 64 amino acids in DNA. The i-Ching Chinese book of changes is made up of 64 hexagrams and functions much like DNA and the Sri Yantra.

Buddhist mandalas depict a circular aura field around the heart and a smaller halo around the head. Two points in the body that create torus vortexes through the flower of life flow of energy.

In Buddhism, the artwork often depicts the Merkaba vessel as a lotus that holds the human jewel (the enlightened human) inside it. This is because a tetrahedral black hole vortex looks like a flower with petals (Flower of Life) around you. It carries you to parallel realities with the same set of people and a similar environment that matches your frequency. This is why it is best to love people as they are and be the best you, you can be. Radiating at this level of inner peace, compassion, and unconditional love will activate your Merkabah, Sri Yantra, or whatever name your spiritual tradition uses to identify the process of matching higher and higher realities. Your external reality matches the frequency your heart is emitting outward into the universe. You know you moved into a new parallel reality when those people you know well suddenly behave differently. Some people's eye color will change for some experiences of traveling within the multiverse in their multidimensional mandala. Moreover, specific details that you previously remembered no longer exist or are slightly different. Some people coming into this awareness of their dominion over reality may even notice slight differences in their neighborhood that they don't remember was there. Often, everyone in the parallel reality that is new to you may think you are forgetful because they live in that current reality and don't know any different. You do not change reality. You jump into new parallel realities that match your unique frequency.

Everything external is just self-projection mirroring your internal frequency. Simple physics. The universe has no choice but to give you precisely what you are and reflect what you feel inside. If you are in peace, then the projected environment will be peaceful. If you are unconditional love, then what projects back to you are loving people and situations. What you send out comes back to you because you are the creator of your own life experiences and each lesson in love moves you into higher realities where others of the same frequency reside. Many spiritual traditions use sacred geometry as symbolic records explaining fundamental metaphysics (quantum physics). Art is an encrypted record-keeping tool hidden in plain sight that supersedes egocentric consciousness. You can see the big picture and instructions when you go above the semantics of separatist consciousness and unify similarities in all relevant traditions.

Nine interlocking isosceles triangles form yantras. Four of them point upwards and represent the female energy Shakti, while the other five-point downwards, meaning the male energy Shiva. Each person has female and male energy inside them, according to the wisdom of the Sri Yantra symbol. When observing the movement of a black hole from the top view, it looks like a Yin and Yang symbol. The Yin and Yang symbols are another form of the Merkabah represented in esoteric traditions. These triangles are not ordinarily composed but have aspects of the Golden Ratio in them. All versions of sacred geometry have the same math compositions.

Just as we have rectangles drawn to the specifications of the Golden Ratio, triangles too have their properties. Triangles have three variants, which are the base length, the slant length, and the height. The angle also plays a significant role. What is impressive is that the Yantra triangle is a proportionate cross-section of the Giza Pyramid, incorporating both unique numbers Pi (3.142) and Phi (1.618) ratio. The base angle of the triangle in the Yantra is seen to be around 51 degrees. The same value was attributed to the base of the Great Pyramid of Giza.

The sacred geometric mathematics of the Sri Yantra suggests that the pyramid structures around the world are also energy conductors. The standard form of the Sri Yantra has nine interwoven triangles and constitutes a total of 43 triangles. Different versions have circles and squares surrounding the triangles, and they are said to form the boundary within which an awakened spiritual avatar typically resides in the intersections.

In the Kabbalistic Tree of Life symbol, it is taught that if one focuses on specific points on the body, they can tap into communication with the different archangels and ascended masters residing at other spiritual placements is shaped like the Tree of Life points. The center of the Sri Yantra has a Bindi (dot), the focus area you can meditate with. The Bindi dot is often placed on the spiritual 3rd eye location on the forehead. The third eye is between your eyes and at the center of your forehead. You can either start from the inside and move out or do it vice versa when you draw the Sri Yantra. The former is seen to be a constructive view, while the latter is a destructive one.

The Sri Yantra might look like a relatively simple design, but the construction is a highly complex affair even with the proper math compasses. The Sri Yantra's main point is that many spiritual traditions are as far back as Zoroastrian, Egyptian, Sumerian, Hinduism, Buddhism, Judaism, Kabbalah, and Gnostic Christianity; a few practices all have the same similar teachings. Yet, each tradition is distinctively different due to the various mystics who taught such teachings through inherited schooled knowledge or receiving cosmic truths by activating their 3rd eye in meditation.

The Sri Yantra from India's ancient Vedic text is older than many modern religions and spiritual traditions in practice today. In Hindu and Buddhist mythology, it is believed that the descendants of the Fertile Crescent and Asia have roots in a mythological enlightened civilization called Lemuria that sank into the ocean from a megaflood over 13,000 years ago. The Sri Yantra three-dimensional temple structure formed from the Sri Yantra symbol is depicted in many Hindu and Buddhist mandalas.

It is believed by students of the Sri Yantra sacred geometry to represent Mt. Meru of Lemuria. The main takeaway is that there are no "chosen" people. There is only one person here, and we are interconnected beings to the one universal mind. You have to choose you, and be the best you, you can be. Everyone else is amazing as they are. Separation is a delusion of the mind. Unity consciousness is the singularity of the cosmic heart. In the research done by the Sri Yantra Geometry Research, they study the concepts and interpretations of what a Sri Yantra is according to the ancient 7,000 years old Vedic text of India from the Indus Valley.

According to modern archaeologists, the Indus Valley civilization in Northern India lasted during the Bronze Age. However, the Rig Vedic Text of the four Vedas that many Hindu scholars credit for the Sri Yantra and the swastika symbol of abundance goes back to over 7,000 – 13,000 years ago. According to Madhu Khanna, he argues that

"The Sanskrit word 'Yantra' derives from the root 'yam' meaning to sustain, hold or support the energy inherent in a particular element, object or concept. In its first meaning, 'Yantra' may refer to any mechanical contrivance harnessed to aid an enterprise. The meaning of the term Yantra has been expanded to refer to religious enterprises and has acquired a special theological significance. Mystic Yantras are aids to and the chief instruments of a meditative discipline. A Yantra used in this context and for this purpose is an abstract geometrical design intended as a 'tool' for meditation and increased awareness" (Khanna, 1979). In short, the Sri Yantra is a meditation tool that is used to attain spiritual awareness.

In the Sri Yantra Geometry Research, this organization explains that the Sri Yantra design is made up of four triangles pointing up with five overlapping triangles that point down. The overlapping of the upward and downward triangles make up the central main image that many are familiar with as the Sri Yantra. Often, the symbol is enclosed in a lotus flower pattern, and the circular energy is further enclosed in a rectangular platform.

The three standard versions of the Sri Yantra are seen as a two-dimensional mandala as often depicted in mandalas of Buddhism, Jainism, and Hinduism. The second command representation of these 64 intersecting points in the Sri Yantra is seen in the three-dimensional pyramidal form to represent Mount Meru's sacred mountain. Mount Meru is believed to be a five-peaked mountain in the Himalayas, considered by many Buddhists, Jainists, and Hindus to be the spiritual center of the universe here on Earth. The last form is the spherical form known as "Kurma," a round energy ball form of the Sri Yantra. Below is a Bhutanese thangka mural of "Mt. Meru and the Buddhist Universe" (Sri Yantra Research, 2020).

As mentioned in the book's introduction, incarnating on Earth is one option out of many eons of incarnations to choose from in the universe. Also, many souls incarnate on Earth to explore what marvelous experiences it holds. Earth is not this horrible planet filled with tortured souls. Although, some people may want others to believe that it is a slave planet. In Buddhism, Earth is a gift. There are not many planets and incarnations where the playing field is leveled through amnesia and the veil placed. This design makes Earth a master class, which allows for mastery of one's Buddhahood with no instructions given. If a soul can find its way to Buddhahood, back to the void, and beyond into infinite love energy, then that person has overcome the game with the universal one-mind experiencing your evolution first-hand as you.

From studying the thangka mural below, you see that Buddhist teachers at all levels in all the universe pops into a parallel reality to teach a lesson and then move on to allow people to practice what is taught. Immersion into one's psyche is evidence of wisdom. When tested, that wisdom does not falter or flip-flop. Truth is always true indefinitely. Earth offers a platform to undo negative karma and earn positive karma towards planning other lifetimes in the cosmic catalog of incarnations to choose from. Souls also have the option not to incarnate in any physical reality at all.

Mathematician and engineer Vladimir Sagmeyster studied the mathematical proportions of the different intersecting points in the Sri Yantra. He then compared the exact points and mathematical distances between the Sri Yantra's intersecting points to our solar system. Vladimir Sagmeyster published his research paper's findings, "Addition to Sri Yantra and Its Mathematical Properties." In Vladimir Sagmeyster's article, he states that "read those two framing lotuses as the indication of an attempt to increase of the Sri Yantra 8 and 16 times. In this way, he revealed a good correspondence between the concentric levels built by him in this relationship of the three Sri Yantra and the orbits of the solar system's planets with a divergence from the real diameters of orbits of about 1.5%. The additional circles in the construction correspond to the boundaries of the asteroid belt and the five trans-Saturnian's planets" (Sri Yantra Research, 2005). Again, we see that in whatever discipline we apply the 64 points of the

Sri Yantra or Flower of Life into the solar system's proportions, we get the same sacred geometry numbers and patterns.

Even mathematically, sacred geometry in the Hindu, Jainism, and Buddhist Sri Yantra, which is often seen in spiritual mandala artwork, we see that all things in creation fit the sacred geometric proportions of Metatron's Cube. Again, I want to note the distinction that I use the name "Metatron's Cube" loosely because the Sri Yantra from the 7,000-year-old Vedic texts is much older than the 1st account of Archangel Metatron in Judaism. Archaeologists and historians still do not know precisely how old the Vedas of India are because much of ancient civilizations that may hold remnants of these sacred geometric symbols may lay underwater.

We only know about these folklores through indigenous mythology about a worldwide megaflood. Many Southeast Asian Buddhist mythology documents in temple murals and literature the oral stories about an advanced Lemurian civilization in the Pacific Ocean. Rumored remnants left from that ancient enlightened civilization lay ruin in pyramids and megaliths on tops of islands throughout the Pacific Ocean, which did not wholly sink underwater with the rest of the advanced society. The Buddhist folklore reports the survivors of Lemuria being scattered all over the Pacific Ocean islands and all overland masses as far away as Asia and the Americas.

In Buddhist mandalas, the lotus symbol is a five-pointed Star of David, a Merkaba vessel inside the Sri Yantra design. It is accompanied by an outer ring and an inner ring. The outer ring is the frame of purification. The inner circles is the process back to enlightenment. The jewel in the center is the person, themselves. This whole structure functions inside a pyramid-shaped frame because the pyramid is a perfect shape like the harmonics, which flows as an energy conductor for the human energy system. In Judaism, this is known as a Merkabah.

Researchers in cymatics research found that playing different hertz frequencies into a sand plate creates a sacred geometry pattern that looks like a Buddhist mandala. Sound frequencies are measured in the form of a hertz. German physicist Heinrich Rudolf Hertz discovered in 1887 through using a radio waves receiver that electromagnetic waves exist. In honor of his work lifetime, the measurement of one cycle per second is revered as a "hertz." Each hertz cycle is standing waves that are the flow of sine waves reflecting at each other, which look like multiple lines of Vesica Piscis (Wikipedia, 2020).

Sound researcher Brian T. Collins does excellent work using the frequency of 432 Hz in music. In Brian Collins's article, "Importance of A=432HZ Music", he found that playing the 432 Hz frequency to someone will harmonize the human body's emotions as measured in medicine. He also found that perfect Fibonacci numbers and Golden Ratios are found in the instruments he uses to see sound made visible when he played 432 Hz frequencies in water. Through his research, he ultimately discovered that our personal and collective reality is a constructed hologram. By playing different frequencies, it produces different sacred geometric mandala patterns unique to the sound.

Further research on the frequency of 432 Hz is explored in the article "Harmonic Mandalas from the Human Voice" by John Stuart Reid and Erik Larson. John Stuart Reid, an acoustic scientist, working in a UK laboratory, and Erik Larson, a US-based design engineer, discovered the 432 Hz is the human voice's frequency. This engineering duo developed a sophisticated CymaScope for cymatics that can take anyone's voice and show the sacred geometry unique to that person's DNA blueprint. Each human being's mandalas are unique to them and show their complete energetic DNA blueprint in sound. It's the genetic code concerning sound. Both men found in their sound research using an electronic CymaScope that everyone vibrates at 432 Hz. The sacred geometry mandala displayed in a CymaScope from the frequency emitted into the tonoscope from the voice of each person has slight differences, which make each of us unique from one another in terms of sound (CymaScope, 2013). The Cymascope cymatic tool created to show what the sound of any frequency looks like in three-dimensional terms shows us that sounds do not travel in waves. Sound travels in bubbles.

In the article "Harmonic Voice Mandalas" by Cymascope, they state that, *"Your voice is a holographic representation of all that you are and contains all aspects of your energetic field. Despite what is taught in schools and colleges, all the sounds around you travel to your ears as beautiful holographic bubbles, not as waves. Sound waves do not exist. The wave model is merely a mathematical concept, and it is not how sound travels. The CymaScope effectively images a slice through the sound bubble of your voice, revealing the beauty within."* (Cymascope, 2013, p. 1-2). The sound researchers found out through the Cymascope technology that every person and every living thing that emits a frequency has a unique sacred geometric mandala pattern unique to it.

Sound does not leave our lips as waves but as holographic bubbles

Like voice fingerprints, every living being is unique no matter how much it looks like another person. The unique sacred geometry mandala unique to everyone shows up in a CymaScope as a three-dimensional bubble. CymaScope refers to these voice signatures as "DNA Voice Signatures." Just as DNA is an identifier of a person's genome's unique genetic markers, DNA Voice Signatures function the same way in having unique geometric markers unique to the person to whom the voice belongs. Suppose you only look at the sacred geometry mandala bubble in a sand plate of tonoscope. In that case, you will see the two-dimensional form of the bubble of sound, which looks like Metatron's Cube or what you often see in Buddhist mandala artworks.

When the researchers of CymaScope sliced open the sacred geometry bubble of sound, they saw that the two-dimensional flat version of the three-dimensional bubble looks like a mandala pattern. I don't know how else to say this if you haven't gotten the point yet, but *every sentient being is sound and light frequencies that is a bubble orb.* Every voice or sound frequency is a bubble made up of energy waves that fit the Phi's exact mathematical proportions, the Pythagorean, the Golden Ratio, and all other sacred geometry math. Every person's bubble mandala is the design of sacred geometry.

So you see, everyone is an equal version of divinity in physical form. Sacred geometry is the smoking gun linking all relevant spiritual traditions together, and it can be proven holistically through cymatics. Therefore, the east's sound chanting in spirituality can be scientifically truthful in their belief that links all of us to one collective family. Every wise man and every wise woman from many ancient religions and spiritual traditions have their version of sacred geometry. As you study them, you see that it is a piece of the more fantastic puzzle. It is just another version of the Sri Yantra symbol. The Sri Yantra symbol is the sound of any sentient being in the form of a cosmic bubble, which a Cymascope has shown in their research. *The Sri Yantra is the sound of a human being and the sound of any living being in nature, which is a sacred geometry mandala when played in a Cymascope. Everyone is a Buddhist mandala.*

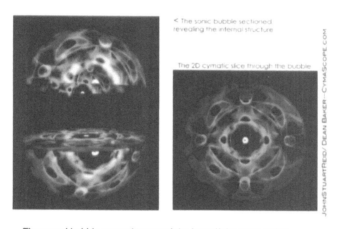

The sound bubble opened to reveal the beautiful pattern within

Another exciting thing that the Cymascope can do is take any human voice and display the unique sacred mandala that the person's voice looks like in two-dimensional designs. Again, each person who has their voice made visible using the Cymascope will show a unique mandala or orb that is distinctively them and not anyone else. The Cymascope shop offers a DNA Voice Signature artwork to the public. When two people's orbs or sacred geometry mandalas are overlaid, it shows the Vesica Piscis. Again, if you turn two-dimensional mandalas into a three-dimensional bubble, it is the physical representation of what every person is in terms of energy. You can order your mandala of your vocal DNA through this website, http://soundmadevisible.com.

Kwan Yin and another female Buddha travel the cosmos in their bubbles.

Sacred Geometry links many mystic spiritual traditions together. This has been proven accurate through cymatics research. The different mandala designs in ancient mystic artworks of highly vibrating people around each person are portraying the Sacred Geometry of their Merkaba(aura). By working on improving themselves through positive thoughts and feelings, these higher frequency people who radiate out a higher level of energy affect the aura fields of others around them positively. By addressing the issues that hold down their energy field, they release struck energy through changing perspectives, which radiate out their true essence.

Another researcher in the field of sound harmonics is Johnathon Goldman. In his work, "Project Om Chart," Jonathon Goldman covers how sound therapy has healing abilities in medicine. He researches frequencies in cymatics and found that sound waves at an "Om" frequency create the Sri Yantra tetrahedral star that encompasses the Star of David, the Merkaba in humans. When Johnathan Goldman tested the 432 Hz into a sand plate or tonoscope equipment, he discovers that the 432 Hz frequency-converted into a Sri Yantra symbol on his sand plate equipment (Goldman, 2012). The name "Om" in eastern chants is the name given to the universal one-mind of the Lord.

This scientific research is worth repeating. The "Om" chant is equal to the 432 Hz frequency of a human voice, equivalent to the Sri Yantra symbol. This is why the tonoscope sand plate translates both the 432 Hz frequency of a human being and the "Om" Buddhist chant as the Sri Yantra symbol in the lab. The Sri Yantra symbol is natural. The Sri Yantra symbol is not artificial. It is a natural formation, according to sound research. The fact that cymatics researchers found that nature displays the Sri Yantra when 432 Hz or the "Om" chant is played shows divinity in creation. Everything in creation is by the design of the universal one-mind.

The fact that everyone radiates at the same 432 Hz of "Om" means that every person, no matter their makeup is a mini reflection of the universal one-mind of the Lord. Everyone is a unique expression of the Lord's consciousness. Let me repeat this important discovery in sound that Johnathan Goldman made.

The 432 Hz sound frequency of a human being is the same as the "Om" chant, which both 432 Hz and the "Om" chant convert into the Sri Yantra symbol. Every human being is a Sri Yantra, is a 432 Hz frequency, is their own "Om," and is a cosmic bubble of sacred geometry. Everyone is energy. Tune it!

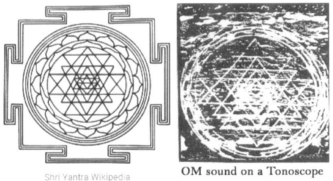

Shri Yantra Wikipedia

OM sound on a Tonoscope

Everything is energy, and the only difference between the different species is the specific sound frequency unique to that species. Cymatic chanting and mantras are often used in eastern and many other spiritual traditions to help balance the harmonics of a person's misaligned energies seeking healing. The Sri Yantra is the cymatic cosmic symbol formed when "Om" is sounded into a tonoscope in sound wave research. The "Om" chant is often used in Buddhism to convey the oneness with God. Even in the sonic study, the harmonics of "Om" say that you are gods and goddess incarnated into physical reflections of the one universal energy source. We are all equal reflections of source energy that resides in each of us. The universal energy inside everyone is waiting for each person to self-realize this and accept others as mirror images of ourselves. We are all working on tuning our own Merkabah.

Yin Yang Symbol

Before I get into the concept of polarity in creation, Yin Yang's definition must first be understood. Wikipedia, Inc does a great job summing the definition of Yin Yang as "In Ancient Chinese philosophy, Yin and Yang is a concept of dualism, describing how seemingly opposite or contrary forces may be complementary, interconnected, and interdependent in the natural world, and how they may give rise to each other as they interrelate to one another. In Chinese cosmology, the universe creates itself out of primary chaos of material energy, organized into the cycles of Yin and Yang, and formed into objects and lives. Yin is the receptive and Yang the active principle" (Wikipedia, 2020). So, in short, remember that the Yin Yang symbol means the balance of opposites, which allow new expressions or creations that rise out of this dualistic force of opposing energy. The polarity journey in which souls incarnate into the physical world such as Earth is made possible because of the polarity caused by the Yin and Yang energies.

The Yin Yang symbol is commonly known as the origination of Chinese philosophy. However, it has been seen in crop circles and many spiritual artworks that reinforce the significance of balance, harmony, and unity as a foundation of polarity. Polarity is the seemingly opposing energy that looks like mirror opposites of one another. Yet, with a closer inspection of the Yin Yang symbol, you see that the light and dark images in the Yin

Yang symbol are mirrors of each other. The light's reflection is seen in the reflection of the dark and vice versa in this symbol. Even further, you see that symbols move towards the right side and coil back around in a circular pattern repeatedly. Where do we see this movement of energy so far in the study of sacred geometry? As you may recall, the movement of energy circulating in a coil pattern is seen in the Flower of Life symbol. When the Flower of Life symbol is mapped out into a three-dimensional structure around people's aura field, it coils into a toroidal energy field, which makes up the human energy system around a living being.

The concept of polarity in the game of life is also reflected in the Yin-Yang symbology. Remember, the symbol has the meaning of dualism or polarity to achieve the same goal of balance. Without the opposite in existence, then neither side of the Yin-Yang of polarity could know of themselves. One must exist for the other to have a mirror reflecting to see its reflection. For example, a man needs to see a woman's existence to know he is a man. The concept of an up needs a down to know that it is up. Good needs to see what is not good and not beneficial to see what is defined as evil. The spirit world needs a physical world in which souls incarnate into to know it is a spirit domain. A person mirrors a companion, reflecting the love they emit outwards back to themselves in the form of another person in a two-way Yin-Yang rotation of love energy.

    For the Lord to know itself, it needed to create a separate identity known as the ego, which everyone plays as themselves different from the universal one-mind. Even the concept of love is an offshoot of the polarity of the ego. For the ego to have that specialness and love at an individual level from one person, it needed to separate itself from the universal one-mind's wholeness to create another being, which reflects love. Through another being, they can feel the mirror reflection of what kind of love they emit outwards.

There needs to be a dualism in the philosophy behind the Yin-Yang symbol. Duality exists in all of life and even in creation. Polarity exists for new creations to bud and to receive recognition of oneself. Let me expand on this straightforward and also very complex philosophy of polarity in creation. For the universal one mind to know itself and experience its creations, it needed to create separatism. Therefore, in the concept of the universal one mind, there is the oneness with the universe.

Whenever someone becomes enlightened and attains Buddhahood through getting reabsorbed into the void or spiritual emptiness of the universal energy of the Lord, they choose to let go of their addiction to playing the most excellent game in creation, creation itself. That person decides to let go of their identity and let go of their ego to become united with the pure energy of the universal one mind's consciousness. The spiritual emptiness or void that Buddhists talk about is the zero point of space. From the flat line hum of the void, polarity shoots out into various expressions of source energy. Beyond the void is the energy of eternal, infinite love energy. Boundless love energy is the heartbeat of the universal one mind.

Very few souls will return to the void to be reabsorbed by the cosmos' universal energy source with the Lord because very few beings will give up their addiction to playing the game of polarity. The game of polarity is magical. Not every soul that plays the games of the Yin Yang in polarity creates suffering for oneself. Many souls in the physical create wonder and even more wonder as far as the angels can see. There is no right or wrong way to explore parallel realities in creation.

When you are ready, you will return to the void. If this interests you, you will return to the void and go beyond the infinite energy of love at some point in your endless existence. However, many Buddhist traditions have reported learning from celestial Buddhas. They incarnated back to the Earthly domain from the void or beyond to help raise the collective consciousness at pivotal moments in Earth's history.

For even the Lord to experience and see its reflection of oneness with all its self-expressions of itself, this energy source needs to have separatism mirror back to itself its oneness. Separatism is the universal one-mind split into multiple facets of itself into unlimited versions of sentient beings in the cosmos. Through splitting off into infinite versions of itself, the universal one-mind sees its one reflection and appreciates its journey back to oneness through the 1st hand experiences of the separate mini versions of the universal one mind.

Therefore, the concept of polarity or dualism through the Yin Yang symbol is a visual representation of how the universe works in its self-expression. So, every sentient being will play in the universal game of polarity in the Yin Yang of creation repeatedly until they decide to return to the oneness and get reabsorbed into the void of the eternal energy source of the Lord.

At some point in infinity, the concept of oneness decides to re-experience its self-expression by choosing to re-enter into another sojourn. The game of polarity provides many options in the Wheel of Dharma. Much like work, play, and long extended vacations until you decide you're done with holidays for a while and want to go back into the game of polarity. A more conscious creator of your mastery will do things they enjoy for work and substance.

In many Buddhist philosophies, this concept of mastery is known as Bodhisattvahood. Bodhisattvas are ascended masters who know how to play the game of polarity and choose to return as awakened individuals to help others live a life creating less suffering for themselves and others to reach enlightenment. The female Chinese Buddha, Kwan Yin, is well known for this type of service.

Further expansion on the dualism or polarity of opposing energies in the Yin Yang symbol is explained well with the Berger Foundation when they state, "Life's oppositions, such as male and female, light and dark, are always in balanced tension. Even within that tension, each term has some of its counterpart within it. Thus, for example, the dark of night has the light of stars within it. This holds even for the opposition of good and bad, especially as applied to the evaluation of events. The Yin Yang symbol represents the interlocking of opposites because every place where a diameter line can be drawn across the circle it intersects both white and black." (Berger Foundation, 2012). In essence, all things in creation have both versions inside it to exist in the physical. The key is to turn the negative into a positive. You transcended the mirror in which the negative fears are a tool to reflect to the user what you want to do next. Does the negativity resonate in your heart? Do you want to explore the negative further or move towards the positive at this time? You'd be surprised how much people love the energy of hate and victimhood because it negates self-responsibility. When the suffering reaches its bottom, many people will get up and walk out of that game or be defeated by it. It's all an exercise to play the Yin Yang game of polarity, most preferably.

Positivity and unconditional love is our natural state always because all of creation is a reflection of source universal consciousness. Negativity is a dichotomous tool of reflection. Negativity can help us decide what we want to create next. This is why negativity continues to separate, divide, and fuel more chaos repeatedly until it makes the creator, you, self-destruct. Suppose you have had enough, then transcend it. Negativity can force you to make choices and actions that fuel positive, loving expansion in your inner being. Without the Darkness, there can't exist light. The spirit world is eternal light.

The physical world has sunsets and sunrises because it offers that divine dichotomy of opposites for Earth to self-create that expression of sunrises and sunsets we all love so dearly. There must be a balance. A middle way, as Buddha would say. Being physical is about creating and living in the now, which is about being in motion towards manifesting your complete piece of art. Your art can be your music, artwork, lifestyle, or anything that brings you joy and excitement about living in physicality.

The point of having a physical body is to be in the act of creation. The Yin and Yang in motion create a spiral pattern to reflect the union of the mind-spirit-body interaction. The spirit feels excitement towards manifesting a new experience, which is felt from the heart. Then the mind starts to think of how to manifest it with the help of your higher self that communicates with the universe and one oversoul to find the quickest, fastest way to navigate the synchronicities or series of events that will lead to the full manifestation. Your body is the final element of the physical reality you exist in. Your body needs to be in motion through doing the required actions to follow through with each opportunity manifesting in front of you in a series of divine events until you blossom into your complete intended real experience.

    Here's another example, men have feminine attributes inside as well as a woman having masculine traits. Dominance is one aspect of the duality of human nature that is unstable and will self-destruct. A balance of polarity or equilibrium in the dichotomy of anything in life is necessary for peace and fruition. That balance of polarity consciousness is the fruition of oneness in the divine. Another aspect of the Yin Yang symbol is that it represents inner harmony in all sentient beings regardless if you're human, humanoid, spirit, or animal.

In the article written by Verna V. Aridon Yater Ph.D. in her article, 'The 50 Primary Universal Laws', she re-states the #1 Universal Law of Harmony that often is noted in the understanding of the Yin Yang symbol in eastern philosophy. The Law of Harmony states, "This law supersedes even the fundamental law of karma, for harmony, is the utmost potential of balance. The purpose of karma is to attain harmony. If you through a rock into a pond, you disturb the pond's harmony. You are the cause. The effect is the splash, and the ripples that flow out and back until harmony is restored. Similarly, your disharmonious actions flow out into the universe and back upon you, lifetime after lifetime, until eventually your harmony is restored." (Yater, 2012). Everyone has a Yin and Yang energy inside of them and in the creation of their lives. Understanding this symbol can help you transcend yourself through finding balance, harmony, unity, and oneness, which is the embodiment of the Yin Yang symbol. Understanding the concept of harmony in the Yin Yang symbol provides excellent insight into the idea of reincarnation and pre-life planning before a soul enters Samsara on the Wheel of Dharma.

According to the Acupuncture Massage College, the Yin and Yang symbol of dark and light opposing energies is used in traditional Chinese medicine as a model of diagnosing and treating illnesses. The emblem first cropped up in the Chinese Book of Changes, the *I Ching*, around 700 BCE (Acupuncture Massage College, 2019). Regarding the *I Ching*, China's ancient Book of Changes, it too is designed much like the Sri Yantra and the Flower of Life in that it has 64 markers in it like the 64 intersection points in the Sri Yantra and

Flower of Life symbols. The school further explains the relationship of Yin Yang in their blog article, "Yin Yang in Traditional Chinese Medicine" (Acupuncture Massage College, 2019, p. 1) as follows. To better understand the concepts of Yin and Yang, it helps to know about their Four Aspects. The Four Aspects describe the relationship between *Yin* and *Yang*. *Yin* and *Yang* are simultaneous:

1. **Opposites**- *Yin* and *Yang* are Opposites. A standard Yin and Yang relationship is day and night. While opposites, they can only be understood as a relationship. For example, Darkness is relative to *Ying*, while *Yang* is relative to Light. The balance between the two is constantly shifting and progressing cyclically.

2. **Interdependent**- While opposite, *Yin*, and *Yang* are interdependent. One cannot exist without the other. Yin and Yang are mutually dependent on each other. One cannot exist

without the other. Everything that has Yin must have Yang, and vice versa.

3. **Mutually Transformative**- *Yin* and *Yang* are constantly in a flux state and affect each other. If one changes, the other follows. Nature, by definition, cannot be static. Just as a state of total Yin is reached, Yang begins to grow. For example, there is no day without night.

4. **Mutually Consuming**- *Yin* and *Yang* are naturally balanced but are continuously changing. The change is typically harmonious but can become imbalanced. There are four possible states of imbalance:

The Four States of Imbalance:
1. Excess of Yin
2. Excess of Yang
3. Deficiency of Yin
4. Deficiency of Yang

Understanding these imbalances of Yin-Yang in the body is the foundation of the root thought used in acupuncture.

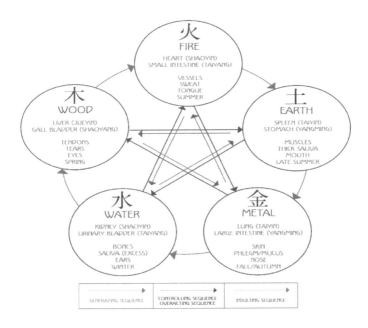

Daniel Weber, Ph.D., MSC, attended medical school at Northwestern University Feinberg School of Medicine and graduated in 1993, having 19 years of medical experience. Additional Orthopedic Surgery training was conducted at the University of Michigan Hospitals and Health Centers. Dr. Daniel Weber discusses the need to have a balanced approach to life in his web seminar, "The Yin Yang Nature of Immunity." Dr. Weber explains that too much excess in each direction may cause an immune imbalance to your overall health.

The Yin Yang symbol has been used in Taoist and Confucius spiritual traditions to represent various ways to understand the flow of energy in cosmology. At the elementary level of understanding the Yin Yang symbol, it is the relationship between opposing energies that need one another to exist in harmony. The concept of polarity is not one of the inner feuds but one of harmonious balance. Too much of the Yin energy cannot express itself fully or know itself without the Yang energy to push against it. Together, the Yin and Yang energies flow like the Flower of Life.

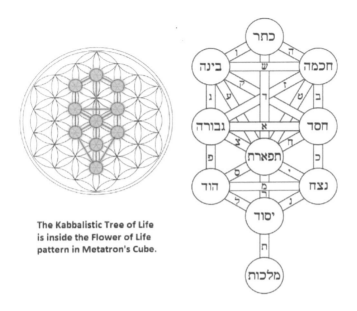

The Kabbalistic Tree of Life is inside the Flower of Life pattern in Metatron's Cube.

Tree of Life

The Tree of Life has shown up in many spiritual traditions and mythological artwork as far back as ancient Egypt, Assyrian, Sumerian, China, Hinduism, Buddhism, Mayan, Judaism, and Kabbalah. In the continuation of further evidence showing that sacred geometry symbols have cropped up well beyond any known religious and spiritual traditions in modern society, the common theme about the nature of the Tree of Life continues to refer to this symbol as a map of the human body. Wikipedia defines the Merkabah as follows, "Merkabah/Merkavah is a school of early Jewish mysticism, c. 100 BCE – 1000 CE, centered on visions such as those found in the Book of Ezekiel chapter 1, or the *heikhalot* (palaces) literature, concerning stories of ascents to the heavenly palaces and the Throne of God. The main corpus of the Merkavah literature was composed in the period 200–700 CE, although later references to the Chariot tradition can also be found in the literature of the *Chassidei Ashkenaz* in the Middle Ages. A major text in this tradition is the *Maaseh Merkavah*" *(Wikipedia, 2020).* The best definition of the Merkaba I have found is from the Jewish mystic tradition, which translates the word to mean "Chariot."

Further research into the same concepts in sacred geometry found in other mystic traditions shows a more comprehensive understanding. When all these traditions are reviewed, the same perspective of the Tree of Life in sacred geometry is rediscovered in the Merkaba grand design. As you can see in Ezekiel's wheel within wheels' religious artwork depicting his description of how the Merkabah rotates, we see an interpretation of intersecting and clockwise rotating circles, which overlaid over each other to form the Vesica Piscis. The image in the fresco of St. John the Baptist Church in Macedonia represents a commonality in how we understand in science the clockwise rotation of how energy flows in a coiling circular motion, as I have explained in the movement of the Flower of Life symbol.

The artwork created in 1670 BCE by Matthau Merian shows his rendition of Ezekiel texts' vision in his vision of what a Merkabah looks like. The artwork indicates that the Merkabah is a light bubble that, upon closer inspection, shows the coiling wheels and geometry inside the wheel.

This is very similar to the known scientific knowledge in DNA research that DNA is made of light particles on a microscopic level. We also know that cymatic study found that all energy sent out through the human voice is the movement of energy in the form of a bubble with the sacred geometry of that person's vocal DNA signature inside the bubble. So the 1670 BCE depiction of Ezekiel's vision is close to our modern science showing that every sentient being is an orb of sacred geometric light traveling from one experience to another into different levels of existence.

Please note Ezekiel's vision from the artwork below because it is him learning from a highly evolved being that sits inside a Merkabah mandala. This will come up again in the rest of the book about master teachers traveling between parallel realities in their Buddhist mandala. Buddhist mandalas, as Merkabahs, are not unique to Asia. Other cultures also have accounts of master teachers traveling in their Merkabahs to teach ways to live life with less suffering.

Copy of Matthäus Merian's engraving of Ezekiel's vision (1670)

Ezekiel's Wheel in St. John the Baptist Church in Kratovo, North Macedonia. Fresco from the 19th century.

In Kabbalah beliefs, the trunk symbolizes the spine and the branches represent the 144,000 nadis that circulate the body. In Chinese energy medicine, this movement of energy up the nervous system, out through the crown chakra, and back around again like a flow of energy moving throughout your body is called "Chi." In Hinduism, this flow of energy coming up your spine and coiling around your body meridians like the flow of energy that the Flower of Life circulates in, "Kundalini serpent." There is one nerve in the human body that connects the whole Tree of Life.

It is the Vegas Nerve. Again, the Vegas Nerve is the only nerve in the body that connects to all seven chakras.

The seven chakras in Hinduism and Buddhism are also referred to as the Tree of Life. It is designed from that Tree of Life diagram. Regardless of the name that each mystic tradition gives the flow of energy that moves in the same fashion around your body, many mystic traditions believe this life force of consciousness is a way for the human being to connect to the spirit world.

The serpent symbol seen in the Caduceus used both by the American Medical Association and in veterinary medicine represents the life force of energy that is believed to be connected to the angels of the spirit world represented by the addition of wings in the Caduceus. According to Wikipedia, "the Caduceus historically is referred to as a Greek mythology symbol about the wisdom linked to a lineage as far back as ancient civilizations of the Fertile Crescent. It's depicted as two serpents of duality leading to angel wings" (Wikipedia, 2020). The Caduceus in medicine is a symbol of a balanced energy field in the body. The Caduceus symbol in medicine has the same meaning as the Yin Yang symbol in Chinese medicine.

In the Caduceus, the two serpents of duality are the flow of cosmic energy flowing upwards through the human body's energy centers. Again, in the Chinese interpretation of the same Chi or Prana energy in Hinduism, the flow of the dark and light energy flows through the five-pointed star's points, representing the human body's main organs.

It's a mystical concept alluding to the interconnectedness of all life on our planet. It is also a metaphor for the connection of humans to the spirit world through consciousness. It's believed by many indigenous spiritual traditions that people can connect to the Tree of Life in the human form through the chakra system. The human chakras are believed to be a vessel of the Merkaba. Again, the Merkaba is the sacred geometric form of the human energy field that cymatic research has shown, which looks like a bubble in the form of energy flowing in symmetry. It looks like unique sacred geometry.

Again, every sentient being is a bubble of sacred geometry or otherwise referred to in Kabbalah as traveling in their own Merkabah. The Merkabah is believed by the Hindu and Buddhist spiritual traditions as an energetic vessel of light that carries sentient beings from one reality to another based on its energy level. The ascending into higher and higher dimensions where many higher beings are commonly referred to as the realms of gods and goddesses by lower conscious beings is believed to be accessed in these ancient traditions through the connection to the spirit world's cosmic tree, which is the Tree of Life. It is also known as the chakra system.

The Tree of Life is believed to be a sacred space design because it is another version of the same sacred geometry. This sacred geometry shows all the planets are aligned in the exact symmetry. Merkaba means a light energy field that will take spirit and body into higher dimensions through consciousness, which travels at thought speed. According to the Gaia article, "What Is a Light Body" by Andye Murphy, the term "Merkaba" is an Egyptian word defined as "Mer (light), ka (spirit), and ba (body)" (Murphy, 2020). So this understanding of a Merkaba is accurate because it explains that everyone is a spirit in the form of a body of light traveling the cosmos.

Often the Tree of Life is represented in ancient artworks from various traditions. It accompanies a metaphoric snake that describes the movement of consciousness of the individual along the different chakras. The knowledge of the different traits of divinity in the Tree of Life point systems and our connection to the angels, which are stationed at different points on the Tree of Life, is accessed by focusing our intentions on the chakra points our bodies.

In Buddhism, a Merkaba is referred to as a "Rainbow Body." The Buddhist understanding of Merkaba is often depicted in Buddhist mandala artwork depicting enlightened Buddhas, which travel different dimensions in a rainbow of light that emanates from the rainbow colors of the human chakra system. These points can also be referred to as dimensions separated by various frequencies within the person's consciousness. Again, the Tree of Life symbol has many names in many mystic traditions.

These ancient knowledge keepers talk about the same concepts of consciousness and how someone manifests their holographic reality within their Tree of Life light body. According to these beliefs, the Tree of Life and the chakra systems are the only reference points. It's believed that one must attain the knowledge on their own by fulfilling the spiritual requirement ordained by the angels in the spirit world to teleport through your consciousness fully.

There's no cheat sheet to enlightenment or ascension of consciousness. No one will save you. You, yourself, must save yourself from a lower consciousness, which manifests whatever reality you perceive. You must complete the introductory courses in "Life" and raise your cellular sine wave frequency to maintain the level of consciousness needed to make such connections. In Buddhism, lower vibrating beings are too unstable to make this connection unless they start using best practices to raise their vibration by releasing negative emotions through forgiveness or transcending them.

The movie *Sex: The Secret Gate to Eden* by Thelma Press covers similar stories covering a wide variety of spiritual traditions from Kabbalah, Western European alchemy symbols, Tantra, Mayan carvings, Tibetan Buddhism, and various

Christian gospels. It also covers the meanings of the Tree of Life in the body and the chakra system. It also demystifies the meanings behind bible stories as allegories that symbolize more complex mystic concepts (Thelma Press, 2006). In this film, Dr. John Dee of the 16th century claimed to connect to the angels by being given the Enochian Alphabet or Language of Angels, which communicates through time and space. He mentions that the angels had to squeeze him to condense his consciousness to maintain the frequency to hold enough consciousness to use the systems he asked to learn. In Buddhist mandalas, the higher the energy of the person, the denser their Merkabah is.

The spine is the body that the Kundalini serpent represents in the Tree of Life. Again, the coined term "serpent" is an allegory portraying consciousness's movement through the chakra system and tree's different points. The serpent's coiling is often referred to as the "Golden Spiral," which can be seen as the double helix coil of the human DNA upon further inspection. A five-pointed star is the Merkaba in the body, seen in the Star of David with the two triangles intersecting. It makes a five-point star of the human form.

In the Yin Yang symbol, the Acupuncture Massage College explains that the Chinese Medicine diagram for the organs is aligned in a five-pointed star. In some traditions, some fruits are used to represent the five-point star of the Merkaba. Apples cut open has a five-point star in it, making it the perfect fruit of sin for mythology. It's believed that there is a light serpent guided by the higher self and a dark serpent driven by the ego. Again, even in the Kabbalah interpretation of the Tree of Life, there is the same Yin Yang interpretation of dark and light energy.

When someone lives with their mind only and not their heart, they live with the ego serpent compared to the light serpent, which lives with the heart guiding the decisions of the mind. Again ego is not an enemy. The ego is a tool of consciousness that allows you to have a unique identity to experience the game of polarity. According to the video, the Tree of Life symbol predates Judeo-Christianity by thousands of years.

Unfortunately, this most sacred Tree of Life symbol in many ancient civilizations and indigenous traditions, which represents healing at all levels, has been misunderstood and lost in common spiritual knowledge. The knowledge of people's divine consciousness through the Tree of Life and chakra system inherent in their DNA has been fractured into multiple pieces and scattered all over various spiritual interpretations. The story of the Tree of Life is fascinating in ancient mythology and modern traditions.

Still, all are pointing to the same original meanings no matter the reference source throughout the world. The essential purpose is that humans are reflections of divine source energy manifested in the physical. People will always be connected to the spirit world. People need to look within to tap into their wisdom and ask for guidance from their angels at times.

Producer Christine Schiavone interviews Stephen Popiotek about the Tree of Life meaning in Kabbalah in this video, "Spiritual Exploration - Kabbalah: Tree of Life." Stephen Popiotek is a metaphysical researcher of the Tree of Life. In this video interview, Stephen goes over the meanings of the Tree of Life in the body. The film explains how juncture points in the body represent different archangel systems in the spirit world and how we may connect to those systems using our advanced consciousness. We do this by 1st awakening into unity consciousness which is an essential requirement for spiritual awareness. Stephen speaks about the Earth ascending into the 5th dimension. His research points to his understanding that two more points may be added to the Tree of Life that is unknown. He thinks the spirit world is expanding since much of humanity ascends into the golden era fueled by unity consciousness.

Again, we see the Tree of Life also shows up in various forms in many spiritual traditions worldwide. The Tree of Life is a design that the universe, the human chakra system, and many other systems in our universe follow. The Tree of Life pattern is one aspect of Metatron's Cube, which has been used by many spiritual traditions worldwide to understand the symmetry in how systems work in nature. It is incredible how the same design can be depicted in so many ways. The universal one mind is so creative is expressing itself in so many-faceted ways. All of sacred geometry show multiple ways to express universal consciousness.

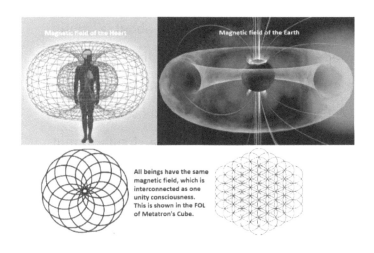

Torus Vortex

To understand what a Torus Vortex is, let's first grasp the definition of what a torus is and what a vortex is. According to Dictionary, a "torus" is defined as "A surface generated by rotating a circle about an axis that is in the same plane as the circle, but does not intersect it. A torus resembles a donut and is a subtype of a toroid" (Dictionary, 2020). Furthermore, Dictionary defines a "vortex" to be "(in Cartesian philosophy) a rapid rotatory movement of the cosmic matter about a center, regarded as accounting for the origin or phenomena of bodies or systems of bodies in space" (Dictionary, 2020). With those definitions stated, the torus vortex is simply a circular donut-shaped movement of energy around the central energy source that is pulling its surroundings towards it. In terms of people, everyone is emitting a strong magnetic field from within their hearts.

That magnetic field around every living sentient being is pulling towards themselves an environment that matches the frequency they are emitting outwards. This magnetic pull phenomenon has been coined as the Law of Attraction, manifesting, birds of a feather flock together, cause and effect, you name it. Many of us have heard of these types of catchphrases to understand the relationship between simple physics. Beings of similar frequency will be attracted to one another. As more similar things align in a common goal, the differences between different groups that radiate at different frequencies will begin to separate into their respective environments. That is the function of a Torus Vortex. There is no judgment. It's simple physics. It is how energy organizes itself.

Every person has a human energy field, which functions like a torus vortex. This toroidal field around the body is what is being depicted in many Buddhist mandalas. This is depicted in much other religious artwork. Often, the toroidal field depicted in spiritual and religious artwork is more prominent around the enlightened person's body. A smaller toroidal field is depicted around the head of the person. The smaller toroidal field around the head is commonly referred to as the "halo" of a person. Below is a typical representation in Buddhist mandala artwork. Every male Buddha and every female Buddha in any reality or dimension within the universal one-mind's consciousness is shown with a large torus field around the body and a torus field for their halo.

Shakyamuni Thangka shows the coiled flow of energy from the Torus fields of Buddhas.

Mathematician Randy Powell had his metaphysical experience at 5-years-old. He grew up trying not to let much of society influence him to unlearn his mysticism and be conditioned by modern religions. He grew up spiritually awakened. His mysticism leads him to do pro-bono work to understand the Abha torus vortex. Randy Powell was a student of mathematician Marko Rodin. Mark Rodin was fascinated by Randy Powell's analytics of vortex math. What Randy Powell did was take the vortex math and map it out on paper. What transpired in math was a picture of the Abha torus vortex. Randy Powell's lifetime of work became the 1st accurate depiction of the Rodin torus in two, three, and four-dimensional models. Following the calculations and proper placement of the numbers creates a torus vortex. Yet, another fascinating way for the expression of sacred geometry in math.

These models help technology researchers see the mathematics in their equipment that they develop. His mission with a fellow mathematician, Marko Rodin, is to work with anyone to help manifest unlimited free energy from the Abha torus vortex. The story of the Abha torus vortex is inspired by research into angel numbers and languages. In Randy Powell's work mapping out the vortex math in this diagram, he found out that it created a torus field by carrying on with the math formula. He goes over his calculations and depictions in his presentation, "Intro to Vortex Math" (Randy Powell, 2010). In terms of math, the proportions of the torus vortex have the proportions of the Golden Ratio.

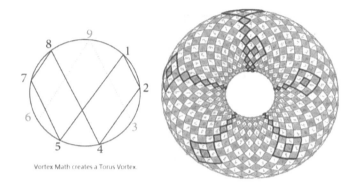

Vortex Math creates a Torus Vortex

The Sri Yantra's math and all the other mathematics derived from sacred geometry. According to the Buddhist traditions, your consciousness creates an opening that functions much like a black hole vortex, which is believed to take you to different parallel realities based on the inner projections you emit outward.

The completed Merkaba vessel that a person travels in, which Buddhists refer to as mandalas, are often two Metta circles. The two circles function much like opposites, but their energy is balanced. Imagine how the Yin Yang symbols would rotate if they were two circles connected to a central area. The energy would rotate in a circular infinite eight pattern and then back up to the other circle in that concept. Again, imagine two balls on top of each other and the flow of energy moving clockwise around the top vortex and making an infinite eight downwards to the bottom torus circle in a counter-clockwise pattern. The flow is the infinity flow of energy. Energy moves in a spiraling black hole within the consciousness of the enlightened being.

The outer circle represents your awakening, and the inner circle represents the process back into enlightenment. The ancient artworks of Metta circles and halos represent the reality of your human circular aura. What is even more fascinating is that Buddhist mystics would depict two layers of circles for the human energy field in many ancient

Buddhist mandala artworks. The image of the legendary female Buddha, Tara, known as the enlightened female of liberation, is depicted with two circles in each aura field. Again, the aura fields of energy are coiled. The one coming out from the heart is always drawn as central in the body's larger aura field. The smaller field of energy emitting from the brain is also depicted in Buddhist mandalas as having two circles. The mandala below represents a different version of Tara traveling the cosmos and stopping along the way to help those who suffer to suffer less through raising their consciousness.

Tara is a female Buddha. She is also a Bodhisattva. Notice the double torus in the halos.

Physicist Nassim Haramein discovered that a toroidal field in any living being also has a double torus. Nassim explains that the magnetic energy field around people has two toroidal fields instead of one large torus. He describes how these fields function in the movie *Thrive* by Foster Gamble. Nassim states, "These toroidal dynamics are visible at various scales. One of them is at the galactic level, which are huge spinning structures with billions of stars. It looks like big arms of galaxies spinning around. They have vortexes that go from the center out to the edge of the galactic halo surrounding them. Stars move from the galactic disk up through the halo, down through the vortexes, and back out again. The Arcturus star has done that path already. That's the appropriate description even for the atmosphere of our planet. The weather goes from the North Pole down to the equator, and then back up from the South Pole up to the equator and then back down" (Thrive, 2011). The description of how a giant torus vortex broke down is two smaller apple-shaped torus vortexes, which have axis points connecting the two apple-shaped torus.

It is a scientific understanding of the same concept of the two circles which make up the Merkaba or mandala, often referred to in Buddhist mandala art. In his statement in the documentary *Thrive* that we all live in an infinite series of cosmos when he states, "Even the dynamics on the surface of the sun are very similar. When you look at the solar system embedded in the galaxy, embedded in the cluster, embedded in the super cluster, we're traveling in this supercluster infinite torus flow" (Thrive, 2011). Through the science of black holes and the flow of energy in cosmology, Nassim explains that these vortexes have bigger and bigger versions of the same thing in the universe.

Every person has the same functioning double tours or two circular rings in Buddhist Mandalas, which live inside the double torus field of the Earth, which lives inside the double torus field of the universe, and on and on it goes. Much like a Mandelbrot set, sacred geometry is mirroring larger versions of itself. The interpretation is that we are smaller versions of the universal one mind, and all reside inside the consciousness of the universal one-mind having our individual experiences in infinity.

In Buddhism, mandalas' concept is that the human body is creating a magnetic pull of energy in this hologram we share. As an energy source coming out from the pull of our hearts, it is believed that people are attracting to themselves their own experiences based on the perspectives of the consciousness of that individual. In modern science, consider the intersecting vortex, which is connecting two double tori's a black hole. Therefore, everyone has a black hole within their hearts that is pulling to themselves their reality. In essence, non-local consciousness enters the top of the funnel through your crown chakra. It moves down through the chakra system and out in a circle back to the crown chakra. This pattern continues to repeat.

In the black hole and sacred geometry research done by Nassim Haramein, he explains how the black hole inside the human heart is the center of the human experience. It is the singularity point where the vacuum torus vortex projects outward and back inward repeatedly to create our projected realities based on whatever we feel inside our hearts. When observing the movement of a black hole from the top view, it looks like a Yin and Yang. Viewing the top of a double torus looks like a Yin and Yang symbol because the energy is doing an opposing infinite eight movement.

Without a three-dimensional rendering of how energy moves between a double torus vortex using 21st-century graphic technology, it is understandable to see how many Buddhist mandalas depict the double torus as two concentric circles. These share the same axis or vortex where the energy movement meets and rotates counter-clockwise in the other bottom torus.

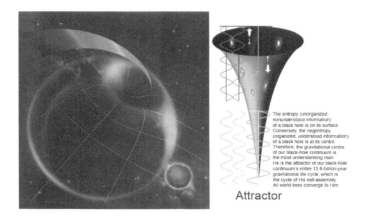

Attractor

The entropy (unorganized, nonunderstood information) of a black hole is on its surface. Conversely, the negentropy (organized, understood information) of a black hole is at its centre. Therefore, the gravitational centre of our black-hole continuum is the most understanding man. He is the attractor of our black-hole continuum's entire 13.8-billion-year gravitational life cycle, which is the cycle of His self-assembly. All world lines converge to Him

Swastika in Indigenous Cultures

The swastika in Asia and many indigenous cultures is an ancient symbol of abundance through awakening to the path of divine enlightenment within oneself is timeless. The swastika still holds its original meaning of "good fortune" in many Asian religions and spiritual traditions. In the Indian Sanskrit language, the word Swastika is broken down as "swa" means "higher self," "asti" means "being," and "ka" means "self." Therefore, according to the Shamanic terminology, the word swastika means "being with higher self" (Shah, 2014, p. 4). Today, many Asian airports decorate their meditation rooms with it.

Many Buddhist, Hindu, and Jainist temples and their parishioners also use the swastika as decoration. This ancient auspicious symbol of enlightenment is not the origination of any such religion or culture. It has shown up in an Indus Valley archaeological artifact, which is believed to date as far back as 13,000 years ago. The swastika is also a symbol of Hinduism from the ancient Indian Vedic text. According to various scholars, the Rig Veda is the four-part Vedas believed to date as far back as 3,000 – 7,000 years ago.

However, the Indian astrology in the Rig Veda suggests that the text may go as far back as 26,000 years ago. The exact age of the swastika is still unknown as much of the history of the Vedas is lost in oral tradition until it was first documented by Sage Veda Vyasa about 3,100 years ago into the four-part Sanskrit Vedic text that we have today (Book Facts, 2020). Before explaining the Vedas' complex history and how the swastika from it factors into the swastika, which influences Buddhism and Jainism's offshoot traditions, let's review all the different cultures that use the swastika as a symbol of abundance and enlightenment.

From my studies of sacred geometry from Buddhist mandalas, the meaning of abundance and good luck for the swastika in Asia is believed to come from the "+" symbol. It is also a representation of the Indian numeral system. The "+" sign is abundant because when you use that symbol, it factors into someone adding more positivity to their life, such as the meaning of "addition" in mathematics. In Asia, the swastika is tilted, and hooks were added, which represents a spiral movement. The spiral movement is meant to show that the abundance is ongoing if someone lives connected to their divine essence within.

That's the original meaning of the symbol as seen to represent enlightenment within. The spiral forward and backward movement of the swastika is a simple representation of the spin in someone's consciousness. They manifest their reality based on their level of energy or frequency. In Buddhism, the left-facing and the right-facing swastika are used to mean different things. Overall, either direction's spin directions are represented to be how someone's human energy field rotates. We have found this understanding of the right and the left spin of the swastika in Buddhism to be correct when comparing it to how a toroidal field within the human energy field works.

As discussed in the article about the torus vortex. Science found that all torus fields have a double torus, layered on top of each other. One torus rotates clockwise, and the other torus within the double torus moves in a counter-clockwise manner. Both double tori make one giant vortex of energy. The human heart and the human brain create a torus vortex. The spin of both *eddies* (*fluid dynamics*) within the human energy field, as seen in Buddhist mandalas, move in the same right-facing and left-facing swastika from the Buddhist interpretation. This is the same dueling movement of the Yin Yang symbol from that discussion of the Yin Yang symbol in this book.

    Furthermore, many Buddhist believe that the "0" symbol that starts the Indian number system represents an "Enso" symbol. In Japanese Buddhism, Enso is the name for a circular form and an expression of enlightenment. Master Buddhist teacher Nagarjuna, the founder of the Madhyamaka school of Mahāyāna Buddhism often practiced in Tibet and India, is revered as such, "whenever he taught in public, *the master would appear as a luminous circle* to reveal the true form of Buddha-nature" (Stevens, 2007). Below is a picture of a monk meditation to the Enso circular symbol of supreme enlightenment. This is the exact depiction from the earlier article about Ezekial in the Bible about receiving messages from a higher being that travels in a circular Merkabah or mandala.

You may recognize this Zen circle where it is believed by Zen Buddhists to encompass a master teacher or Buddha inside it. The circle that a master travels in, according to Zen Buddhism, is very bright and vibrant. You may recall all the various Buddhist Mandalas' images with the master teacher Buddhas traveling in their bubbles. Remember, their bubbles are also known as their Merkaba or Aura. The number zero in Indian number systems represents enlightenment. Zero can also be the spiritual void, and from it comes the game of polarity in the earlier discussion about the significance of the Yin Yang symbol.

The other numbers after zero are 1, 2, 3, 4, 5, 6, 7, 8, 9. The Indian numerical system was introduced to Arabic mathematicians, who later presented it to Europe. In Europe, algebra was created out of the Indian numerical system (Wikipedia, 2020). In Buddhist, Hindu, and Jainism philosophies, the numerical system is another form of seeing the journey of Samsara. "Samsara" is the journey that a soul makes in the reincarnation process. Samsara means to journey.

It is the cycle of death and rebirth until a soul reaches nirvana. It gets reabsorbed into the infinite void of the universe's universal one-mind for infinity—eternal Enso. Beyond Enso is endless love energy. The maker of all life itself. Therefore, the additional numbers represent more abundance added until someone decides to return to infinity and get back to Enso. It is further noted, many Buddhist traditions use the swastika as one of the symbols to represent the 1st Buddha, Gautama Buddha. The swastika is also used for all the other Buddhas that followed. Buddhist artwork will adorn the chest, hands, feet, and heart of Buddha with the positive swastika symbol in Asia. The Indus Valley numerical system understands how our holographic reality works out of the void of zero.

Scholars of Hinduism tracked all the swastika origins back to the Aryan civilization, where India's Vedic spiritual text was originally dissimilated throughout the world from. The enlightened beings of high consciousness from India's Aryan Indus Valley civilization had renowned sages such as Brahman, Vishnu, and Shiva, to name a few. When looking at the Vedas closer, the oldest part of the Vedas is the Rig Veda. In the Rig Veda, the text discusses the Indian astronomy system. This section of the Vedas describes a precession of the equinox as one lunar cycle of "Nakshatra." There are 960 years in one Nakshatra, and there are 27 Nakshatras in the Rig Vedas. If only one procession has occurred and subtracts 2,000 years AD, the Rig Vedas date maybe 25,720 BCE (Book Facts, 2020). In science, it is true that lunar stations have 27 or 28 segments and that it takes 26,000 years to complete one precession of the Earth's axis.

Wikipedia states that a lunar station "is a segment of the ecliptic through which the Moon passes in its orbit around the Earth. The concept was used by several ancient cultures as part of their calendric system. In general, though not always, the zodiac is divided into 27 or 28 segments relative to the fixed stars – one for each day of the lunar month (A sidereal month lasts about 27.3 days). The Moon's position is charted concerning those fixed segments. Since the Moon's position at the given stage will vary according to Earth's position in its orbit, lunar stations are an effective system for keeping track of the passage of seasons" (Wikipedia, 2020). Therefore, according to the Rig Vedas, the Indian astrology and astronomy may be much older than the debated 7,000 years ago where the swastika symbol originates from. According to the Hindu Vedas, the swastika symbol means good fortune and is an auspicious symbol of abundance.

After the earliest dates for the accounts of the swastika symbol were traced to the Aryan civilization in the Indus Valley and the Vedas of India in the Indus Valley, the symbol of good continues to show up in other societies afterward. According to Binpin R. Shah of the research article, "Swastika Was Used in Neolithic, Bronze, and Iron Age Cultures. Its Probable Origin is from Astrology," he states, "The first known archaeological Swastika was [Mezine Swastika.] The earliest swastika ever found was uncovered in Mezine, Ukraine, carved on an ivory figurine, which dates to an incredible 12,000 years, and is one of the earliest cultures known to have used the swastika was a Neolithic culture in Southern Europe. The area that is now Serbia, Croatia, Bosnia, and Herzegovina, known as the Vinca Culture, dates back around 8,000 years" (Shah, 2014, p. 1). Many more uses of the swastika symbol in many ancient civilizations, from pottery as old as the 2,600 BCE Majiayao Culture in China. The 2,700 BCE Minoan civilization had pottery decorated with the swastika symbol. The 5,000 BCE bowls of Mesopotamia were also decorated with swastikas.

Even today, the swastika symbol of goodness is passed on the tradition in the Navajo ceremonial décor. The symbol is used in the ceremonial decorations of the Mayan Indians of Mexico (Shah, 2014). The swastika symbol links many indigenous cultures from many continents to an unknown lineage in the ancient past that no one truly knows about. It is a symbol beloved in spiritual practices in some Native American tribes, indigenous Mayan tribes, and many ancient Vedic-influenced civilizations.

In 2007, archaeologist Dmitriy Dey discovered the Kazakhstan geoglyphs using Google Earth. He found 260 geoglyphs which could only be seen from a satellite view or from up high in the sky. Some of the Kazakhstan geoglyphs are crop circles, squares, giant animals, and swastikas. NASA is investigating the 8,000-year-old geoglyphs of Kazakhstan because they are far more ancient. There are so many more of these human-made mounds, divots, and trenches than the 1,500 Nazca Lines in Peru. The 250,000 meters wide Ushtogay Square Kazakhstan geoglyph has four sides, each of which is as long as an aircraft carrier (MacDonald, 2015). As you can see from the evidence of ancient geoglyphs and ancient archaeological artifacts, the swastika symbol has been around the Indus Valley, all around Asia, and in Central Asia as far back in history as 13,000 years ago. However, the exact dates, how old this symbol is, and how widely it was used in various indigenous civilizations are still unknown.

Even in the study of Faraday waves, the swastika is a symbol that shows up in nature. The swastika is not human-made. It is a natural formation. English scientist Michael Faraday conducted ground-breaking research on electricity. His research discovered that the magnetic field around a conductor carries a current, which established the physics's electromagnetic fields. Electric motor technology was developed from this research. Upon his investigation, Michael Faraday discovered that "are nonlinear standing waves that appear on liquids enclosed by a vibrating receptacle. When the vibration frequency exceeds a critical value, the flat hydrostatic surface becomes unstable." (Wikiwand, 2020). He published his research of Faraday waves in 1831 in the article, "Philosophical Transactions of the Royal Society of London." Michael Faraday found out that fine-tuning the vibrational frequency and acceleration does create diverse sets of symmetrical patterns in nature.

One striking pattern in nature is the swastika, as you can see in the below image. Also, it is worth mentioning that alligators make Faraday waves on the water with their low-frequency lung sounds to call to nearby mates (Wikiwand, 2020). The swastika is a symbol in nature created at specific frequencies, so many spiritual Asian traditions still revere it as an auspicious symbol. The symbol is not a human-made creation by any mystic or civilization, but it is a natural phenomenon.

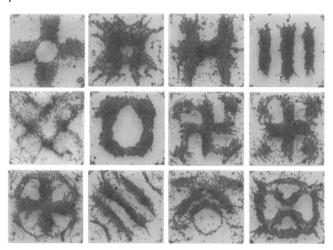

Now that the swastika has been established as an ancient natural symbol of a specific frequency that creates natural patterns, which many traditions have recognized worldwide as auspicious and good, let's understand how Native Americans in the United States see this symbol. It is still widely used in their spiritual practice. The article "Melissa Cody's Whirling Logs: Don't You Dare Call Them Swastikas" explains that the commonly referred to swastika symbol is used as a positive symbol by Navajo and many other Native American tribes around the Mississippi area. It goes far beyond the time of Christopher Columbus "discovering" America. For many Native American tribes of North America, the swastika symbol has long been called a "whirling log," The symbol is seen as meaning abundance, prosperity, healing, and good luck. It holds the same meaning as the swastika in Asia.

The swastika is a broken cross symbol that Native Americans represent the sun, the four directions, and the four seasons. According to

Navajo sand paintings, the rotating cross is often depicted in Navajo artwork as a central marker of the "Yei" spirits' energy. The Yei deities are highly evolved beings that many Native American tribes pay respects to as deities that taught harmony with nature. Masked dancers are used in ceremonies to communicate with the Yei deities as an ancient practice descending from the ancient Mound Builders of North America. (Indian Country Today Media Network, 2013, p. 1).

In the article "Yei Symbol" by Navajo tribeswoman and historian Melissa Cody, the Yei symbols can vary to represent different deities that come through in an auspicious whirling or rotating log pattern. The article states, "A special kind of Yei deity is the Yei'bi'chai. The Yei'bi'chai deity is revered as a "talking God" who can speak to a human directly, telling them how to live in harmony with all living things. This Yei deity also provides some simple rules of behavior to conserve and only use the necessary things to survive.

Because of this advisory role, this Yei spirit is known as the grandparent spirit. The "Rainbow Kokopelli" is a Yei deity who commands the rainbow, giving beauty to all those in harmony. It is thought that his sack was made of clouds full of rainbows or seeds. The "Rainbow Kokopelli" represents the Yei symbol of harmony (Cody, 2013, p. 1). Even in the Native American spiritual traditions for a connection to the spirit world and connection to nature, the swastika or whirling log has the same meanings as many other indigenous cultures worldwide have about this ancient symbol.

The meaning of highly evolved Buddhist teachers riding between parallel realities in mandalas, Ezekial from the bible's accounts of his teachers in a Merkabah, the Zen teachers riding in spinning Enso, and the whirling logs of the Native American Yei spirits all have the same meaning. The meaning is that highly evolved beings travel in a chariot (swastika). This knowledge of sacred geometry Merkabahs has not changed in history or from culture to culture throughout time. Again, the Native American perspective on the whirling log symbol is seen as an auspicious rotation of energy, which the highly evolved Yei spirits travel through. The Yei deities have talked to the people and advise Native Americans on living in harmony by not taking more than they need from the Earth. This is much the same interpretation about the awakened and enlightened master teachers, which incarnate from the spirit world into our physical reality to teach enlightenment to spiritual seekers in Buddhism.

There is still not much known about the Mound Builders of the Mississippi area in the United States. Reverence to the Yei enlightened beings in Native American traditions can be linked back to storytelling and backed up with artwork in Yei symbols to the Mound Builders. We know about the Mound Builders that they were a Native American tribe who, during an estimated 5,000-year timespan, constructed earthen mounds for spiritual practices. Archaeologists believe that the Mound Builders existed from 3,500 BCE to the 16th century and lived in the Great Lakes, Ohio River Valley, and the Mississippi River area (Wikipedia, 2020). The Dakota Native Americans, the 1st Nation Tribes of North America, and many more Native American tribes use the Yei symbol.

There is plenty of physical evidence of the swastika in central Asia and the Indus Valley civilization going as far back as 13,000 BCE. What is known is that this auspicious positive symbol is revered by many indigenous tribes and ancient cultures from the North American continent in the use of the swastika symbol in Native American spiritual traditions. The swastika symbol is also revered as an auspicious spiritual symbol in Mayan and Aztec ceremonial artwork. The symbol carries the same symbolism in many ancient European cultures, which carry on into modern times.

Chapter 3

What is Consciousness?

"Our original nature is...void, omnipresent, silent, and pure; it is a glorious and mysterious peaceful joy - and that is all. Enter deeply into it by awakening yourself."
—Huangbo Xiyun, Zen Buddhist Monk
Authored, *Doctrine of the Universal Mind*

Consciousness in Buddhism is the infinite essence of the one Buddha mind. The one Buddha mind is the consciousness of the universe. Some people in many religions call this universal consciousness "God" or "Allah." Many people in science call this universal consciousness that resides in all creations "the unified field." It does not matter what labels refer to the single consciousness of the universe, which plays different roles directly as independent figurines. We all talk about the same universal mind. It does not matter if one believes in the one being or not because every sentient being is playing its dual nature in the realm of existence. Even atheism is acceptable because to know oneself is also to recognize the lack of recognition in oneself. For the mind of Buddha to realize itself, it split itself into many forms. That spit created polarity or otherwise understood as opposites.

In Buddhism, it is believed that the one universal mind of all consciousness is the principal Buddha head of all mini Buddhas in all the realms. Remember, a Buddha is anyone who awakens to the holographic reality, which responds to the commands of its user. An ascended being is an awakened Buddha who radiates at higher energy levels because they are a conscious creator within the matrix. Buddhahood is available to anyone. There are no initiations, no payments, no organization to pledge allegiance to, no expulsion, nothing is required to join Buddhahood. Buddhahood is living as a conscious creator within the hologram until you release ego upon your last days as a human being and move beyond the void into eternal love energy with the main Buddha.

In the meantime, do your best to cause less suffering and relieve other sentient beings' suffering. You can see the cosmic Buddha-head in science. In science, when a Mandelbrot fractal of repeat patterns in nature reoccurs repeatedly, one outcome is a Buddhabrot. A Buddhabrot is a Mandelbrot set that forms the shape of a Buddha. The universe is so creative in its many forms of self-expression for itself. The below image is a Buddhabrot.

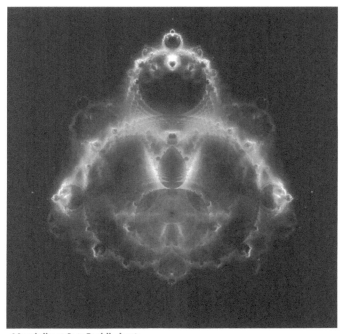

Mandelbrot Set: Buddhabrot
Creative Commons CC0 License. Wikimedia Commons

For one side to know itself, it needed a polar opposite to reflect its interests. From seeing both sides, it created a dichotomy. The dichotomy is a truth that is known from that challenge of opposites. That challenge is the energy that fuels growth and buds into new and newer experiences. Like the Mandelbrot sets in creation, the one Buddha mind continues to create, recreate, create, and recreate into the eons with the game of polarity. The one universal mind is existing in one position. It also exists in the opposing position. It superimposes positions that encompass the whole of polarity. There are many expressions of the universal essence of the Buddha's mind. This singular essence resides equally inside all men, all women, all animals, all spirits, angels, archangels, and sentient beings. All of creation is connected to the consciousness of the main Buddha. Whenever a human being at the bottom of the incarnation scale below archangels and others in creation reaches Buddhahood, that act uplifts themselves and everyone else in the pyramid of creation. All of Samsara moves up a little more away from a lower, denser reality out of ignorance. Metatron, YeshuaH, Kwan Yin, Siddhartha Gautama, Tara, Maya, and so many others in history became avatars.

The Lord expresses itself in various creations to know itself through 1st hand experience. Christ (crystalline) consciousness gets to experience in the viewpoints and experiences of all its creations. The game of polarity ceases to exist once a sentient being realizes the holographic nature of our polar reality by understanding how to engage with how the energy of the soul works. Being self-aware of the responsive nature of our contrasting reality is what many Buddhists consider a spiritual awakening. Raising your consciousness level to the different energy levels until you reach Buddhahood is what Buddhists believe the ascension process. Buddhahood is the level in the physical body of someone who is self-aware in the polar game. The realization is that they are ready to surrender their ego back to the universal mind of the one Buddha and reabsorb back into the original essence of the one mind of the universe.

The "ego" is what Buddhists call the lower level mind in each sentient being, which allows it to have its own independent experience in the game of polarity. So lifetime after lifetime, the ego has fun experiencing the different expressions of God. Once the user has enough and wants to be reunited with God in the void of the universe's singular mind, they let go of their ego, which has served their soul as all these different incarnations over multiple lifetimes. What this process is called is Ego death in Buddhism. This void that some souls achieve by reaching Buddhahood is called in Buddhism "spiritual emptiness." Since time does not exist in the universe's concept of metaphysics, then when a sentient being is ready to return to the void, it is welcomed to reunite with the one Buddha mind.

No matter what, the one mind of universal consciousness is experiencing itself in all manifestations regardless of physical or non-physical forms. Upon the final doorway at the void, every person is tested to see if they are ready to let go of their addiction to creation. The last call is hearing the cry of eons of humanity living in suffering out of their deeds. Many enlightened teachers descend back once more to offer a dharma talk to help reduce suffering before moving onto a new parallel reality. The Yei spirits in the Native American swastika (whirling logs) are much like the Bodhisattvas in Buddhism.

It all comes down to consciousness. Consciousness is the realization of oneself. Recognition of others as aspects of oneself is being conscious about the fractal nature of our Earthly experience. Shifting perspectives is what changes the energy of the user in the game of polarity. As a result, the user moves to a matching parallel reality. You never change what's in the mirror. By changing your smile, the reflection in the mirrors smiles back at you. That is how parallel realities work. You only change your perspective on things. The change in attitude changes your level of consciousness, which the reflected reality is the one that matches you best.

Buddha: Sanskrit word from "budh". Means to "awake". - Dictionary

Consciousness & Oneness

To understand what "consciousness" is, it is helpful to define it. It is given closer inspection to see if it is an accurate perspective in the greater reality by defining a concept. According to the Dictionary, consciousness is "the state of being conscious; awareness of one's existence, sensations, thoughts, surroundings, etc." (Dictionary, 2020). Therefore, there are two parts to being conscious. The first is to be aware of your existence. The second part of consciousness is to be self-aware of the external reality in which a person exists.

In Buddhist studies, my lifelong understanding of consciousness from my spiritual tradition of Buddhism is that every sentient being in the universe is a fractal split of the one universal mind, which resides inside everyone. Every person, animal, plant, and anything in the cosmos has an individual identity experiencing its incarnation as a spirit or soul having a human experience for its evolution. Through a person's consciousness of self, the one universal Buddha or one universal mind often referred to by many Buddhist traditions is also experiencing itself through *being **you**. Let that sink in.*

The Lord Buddha is inside every woman, man, child, animal, plant, and everything. So when someone hurts someone else, they are hurting themselves. It is a Buddhist tradition. There is only oneself. Everyone is a split of the universal one mind and connected to the whole of the cosmos. In Buddhism, the concept of reincarnation and life planning before incarnating on Earth is a serious and fun event that many people in Asia regard highly. Many Buddhists try their best to live their life in a manner that does not create negative karmic debt. Negative karma is unbalanced energy often tied to unresolved discord created in a previous lifetime, which resurfaces in their current lifetime. On the flip side, many Buddhists do their best to make good karma, so they are given good options in pre-planning their next life when they are in the spirit world with their Life Planner and others who help guide their next incarnation. At the very least, practicing Buddhists try not to create suffering.

The concept of reincarnation and working with the Wheel of Dharma is a fascinating topic that many Buddhist philosophers debate. Overall, the consensus among Buddhists is that "consciousness" is the one universal mind. Everyone is a mini

Buddha in the making and will return to the one Buddha upon enlightenment. Afterward, the game of life carries on to other game boards for infinity. Below is a Buddhist mandala artwork about the Buddhist concept of consciousness. It depicts how the self's consciousness leads to a realization of the overall consciousness within the one universal mind of the Buddha.

Kagyu Refuge Tree shows oneness of all Buddhas in all dimensions in the Tree of Life.

Now let's evaluate how the Buddhist tradition views consciousness and what modern science discovered in their research regarding consciousness. In his relationship counseling practice, Dr. Harville Hendrix discusses brain research discoveries that explain how the human brain cannot tell the difference if someone is hurting themselves or hurting someone else who exists outside of them. In lab experiments, researchers hooked up two people's brains and evaluated what happens to the brain when one person says and does hurtful things to the other person who is also hooked up with EEG brain measuring equipment.

Researchers repeated this experiment in multiples ways, and the same results came out. The brain scans of both participants light up in the same areas of the brain. Dr. Harville Hendrix concluded from this brain research that according to the human brain, the human brain could not tell the difference if someone is hurting themselves or hurting another person who exists physically. The pain that one person inflicts onto another person is also felt in the brain of the person inflicting the harm onto another person. This is the foundation of what he teaches in his marriage and relationship counseling private practice.

In the Consciousness Series interview done by Jan Fisher with Dr. Harville Hendrix with the Institute of Noetic Sciences regarding his book, *Getting the Love You Want*, Dr. Hendrix says, "Connection is our nature. That is what we are. We are a connection. There is no such thing as separation. There is no such thing that is something outside or not connected. The difference is that in the cosmos, as well as in you and me and everyone else, the connection is a reality that you can't change. It is a reality that you can lose awareness of. You can lose the fact that you are connected, and that happens when you are anxious. What happens when you are anxious, then you become self-absorbed. When you become self-absorb, then you no longer become self-aware of your connection to yourself sometimes, and to everyone, and everything. Connection means that which we are, and I have this discussion with couples. Connection is joy. Joy is a connection. That's our nature. We are part of the universe. That's what I work with" (Consciousness Series, 2011). Even in Dr. Harville Hendrix's lifelong work in relationship counseling, he uses the science behind brain research to explain to his clients that they are connected. They are the same one consciousness having a dual experience through coupling to understand themselves further.

Dr. Hendrix explains that the understanding of cosmology in how the universe works is much the same structure as how the human brain behaves, which can be used to understand how to have more positive relationships with one another in any relationship. He works with couples to get to a point in how they connect by teaching new ways to communicate, interact cohesively and harmoniously instead of friction.

Another notable field of research in Consciousness Studies comes from the distinguished work of Richard R. Hawkins, MD, Ph.D. Dr. Hawkins's medical expertise comes from his lifelong pursuit to help alleviate people's suffering in mental health. He was a director at North Nassau Mental Health Center (1956–1980), a researcher from 1968-1979 at Brunswick Hospital on Long Island, and his clinic was the most extensive practice in the USA at the time. Dr. Hawkins also co-founded many psychiatric organizations. Notable mental health organizations are the Editorial Board of the Journal of Schizophrenia and the Attitudinal Healing Center in New York. Dr. Hawkins received many lifetime achievement awards in the field of medicine (Veritas Publishing, 2017). Dr. Hawkins devoted much of his life to medicine, and he developed ground-breaking kinesiology methods to map out the level of energy in any living being. The level of energy emitted out from any living being is what he terms the level of consciousness, which someone is. Kinesiology is a muscle test. When used appropriately, it works because all sentient beings in creation share the same lifeline to the mainstream of consciousness from the universal mind of the Lord.

The most significant legacy that Dr. David R. Hawkins left from his lifelong medical contributions, which are plentiful, is the "Map of Consciousness." The Map of Consciousness is a scale of consciousness that every living thing in the cosmos has. Dr. Hawkins explains his technique on how anyone can measure the level of consciousness in his 1995 book, *Power vs. Force: The Hidden Determinants of Human Behavior*. Dr. Hawkins spent much of his medical career in mental health and psychiatry developing a kinesiology technique to ask any question he wanted about anything in the cosmos and all of existence. He got a "yes" or "no" answer directly from the one universal mind because everyone is directly connected to the consciousness of the universal one-mind.

In many religions, they would call this overarching persona that resides in all sentient beings in the universe as the Lord or God. Dr. Hawkins discovered from doing kinesiology muscle testing on integrity that it did not matter who he tested out his questions on. He always got the same calibration results as to what level of consciousness the sentient being resides at. He calibrated thousands of animals, people, plants, and a multitude of questions about the universe.

He discovered that the scale of consciousness could calibrate up to 1,000 points, which is what spiritual avatars like Siddhartha Gautama, Yeshua, Kwan Yin, Moses, Vishnu, and many other enlightened beings in history achieved. Researchers discovered that different people have different energy levels in science and that no two people emit the same energy frequency. Don't be fooled or follow a wolf hidden in sheep's clothing. Dr. Hawkins calibrated top spiritual gurus, priests, deacons, and spiritual teachers with millions of followers multiple times. Many of them did not even meet the essential calibration of, 200 which is the entry-level benchmark for integrity.

This difference in intensity is what Dr. Hawkins explains is why different people emit different levels of energy. In his book *Power vs. Force*, everyone is born into their existence at a certain level of consciousness. How they live their lives and their pursuit of ascending their level of consciousness raise their calibration level (Hawkins, 1995). Many religious leaders sought out the published books about consciousness and calibrating energy levels between different people in our society. Before Dr. Hawkins's death, he was a spiritual advisor and calibrated many spiritual leaders from the Catholic diocese to the Karmapa in Tibetan Buddhism. The Map of Consciousness and kinesiology research provides further evidence that everything in all time and dimensions is interconnected as one universal mind of the Lord. Dr. Hawkins spent much of his later years lecturing about his research. Oneness is consciousness. Consciousness is oneness. Awareness of the oneness within all beings is consciousness. This is expressed in one individual and all people.

Another scientific approach to understanding the consciousness within all beings can be deduced from studying how physical matter is a combination of a wave phenomenon and vibration. One of the earliest cymatics research was demonstrated by Swiss medical doctor, Hans Jenny who published his findings that all physical forms are energy in the form of condensed wave patterns in his 1967 book, *Cymatics: The Study of Wave Phenomena*. Dr. Hans Jenny used his electronic tonoscope to show that when specific vibrational frequencies play into a tonoscope with fluid on top of it, what is created are life-like physical forms (Volk, 2009).

In the article, "From Vibration to Manifestation: Assuming Our Rightful Place in Creation" by Jeff Volk, he states this about Dr. Hans Jenny's cymatic research, "*The similarity between these [standing wave] patterns of resonance and the forms of flowers, plants, and animals, hints at the universality underlying manifest creation. We are witnessing the processes that bring these forms into offering us penetrating insight into how an elaborate web of vibrations interacts to create the world we perceive*" (Volk, 2009, p. 2). Studying and evaluating Hans Jenny's sound research proves that all plants and animals are a combination of standing waves oscillating at a specific frequency. This shows us that there is one universal field of energy that resides inside all animals and plants.

Researcher Jeff Volk continues to state that, "This research has been repeatedly demonstrated using an accepted scientific methodology in enigmatic experiments that attempt to isolate and define subatomic particles, which appear as particles when searched for as such, but as waves of energy when approached with that expectation. From this perspective, *one can begin to perceive the world as a vast interlacing network of discreet fields of oscillation, which become "things" as they interact with the pulsations of our perceptual senses, which are also subtle vibrational fields"* (Volk, 2009, p, 3).

After evaluating the sound research of Dr. Hans Jenny in his book, *Cymatics: The Study of Wave Phenomena* and evaluating the analysis of Jeff Volk, I agree that the hard evidence leads us to conclude that matter is energy. All energy is vibrating at different levels of frequency. Once a person perceives and looks at an oscillating energy functioning pattern into a form, it becomes real to the perceiver. *Therefore, as discovered by Dr. Hans Jenny, all physical reality is a hologram and not truly real. Reality is a hologram as perceived by the user existing within a matrix of perception.* In cymatics research, the unified field of energy that flows in all creation is the exact source of energy that flows in all people. Therefore what cymatics research tells us is that all people are interconnected as one life being connected to the field of the universal one mind. This is a perspective held by many Buddhist traditions and shown in Buddhist mandala artwork.

In Buddhism, many Buddhist master teachers teach about reality as a reflection of what you radiate inside you. The 1st Buddha, Siddhartha Gautama, often spoke about the nature of reality as a reflection of the energy you radiate at. *Siddhartha held many lectures on how the external reality can be changed by doing the inner work on yourself, which results in you experiencing a new external parallel reality different from the one you previously existed in before a change in perception occurred.*

In the lecture "I See You in Me and Me in You" by Thich That Nhat. Thich explains that being conscious of your creation's nature as manifested as uniquely you is also a mirror of the other person looking back at you. In essence, it is another reflective mirror of themselves. Nhat is an exiled Vietnamese Buddhist Monk who is an author, a poet, and a peace activist that lives in France at his Plum Village retreat center. Thich That Nhat was a personal Buddhist advisor to the late Dr. Martin Luther King Jr. regarding peaceful activism during the Civil Rights movement in the United States.

Since his young adult days as a spiritual advisor to Dr. Martin Luther King Jr., Thich continues to lecture and write on Buddhism and reality. Nhat is the author of *Jesus and Buddha as Brothers, Living Buddha, Living Christ, Transformation and Healing*, and many more books. The "I See You in Me and Me in You" lecture explains how the Yin Yang symbol represents our oneness with one another and how we are all interconnected in this hologram.

In this famous lecture, Thich says, "I see you in me, and I see myself in you. *This teaching is unambiguous in the Buddhist tradition.* This teaching is also available in other traditions like Christianity and Judaism. We know that is the trinity. The father is in the son. The son is in the father. The Holy Spirit is in the father. The father passes by the Holy Spirit. When the son looks at the father, he sees himself in the father. When the father looks at the son, he sees himself in the son." (Plum Village, 2017). Everyone you interact with is just a reflective aspect of yourself. What you don't like about them is what repressed issues you have about yourselves.

Acceptance and forgiveness is the more harmonious way to transcend stuck energy and then decide what you want to do next in a relationship. Look in your heart to determine what solution resonates most peacefully in your consciousness. *Often, letting go of the anger that someone did a hurtful act to you is the best present solution. Two people suffer. You suffer as a result of the harm. The other person suffers from not knowing any better and continuing to act poorly out of ignorance.*

There are two ways to practice love in action in this case. You love yourself enough to let go of the anger you hold, which releases you from carrying on this pain. Also, you release unconditional love to the other person by letting them know that you release them of your anger, which is the act of forgiveness. You wish them much love in their journey to get the healing they lash out for through harmful acts upon other souls.

Also, you send love to them to carry on their lessons with the hopes that he or she eventually learns from the error of their ways. However, letting go of the anger over what happened to you by the other person(s), how it happened, when it happened, and all the other factors in the hurtful relationship is the hardest thing to do as well. Some people would instead hold on to the repressed anger disguised as hate and let it wither away their life force until it forms into an illness in their body or makes multiple layers of havoc in people's lives.

There are many ways to understand scientifically that all beings in the universe are interconnected as one universal being within the same consciousness of the universal one mind. It is esoteric, but it's true. There are levels of consciousness. The consciousness of self, the collective consciousness, and the universal one-mind's consciousness are you, him, and herself. All are separate individuals as much as all are in all of the cosmos depending on the perspective you want to see yourself and the all-ness.

This is what many Buddhists, Hindus, and mystics throughout the ages have rediscovered as they become more aware of their enlightenment and learn to play with parallel realities. As spiritual seekers remove one blockage and raise their frequency and consciousness, they become more aware of reality's holographic nature. Such highly evolved mystics begin to become conscious creators of their reality and become mindful contributors to the collective consciousness's reality. It is these highly calibrated people on our planet that are the most powerful in our reality. These visionaries affect the picture quality of the matrix in which many in that reality experience.

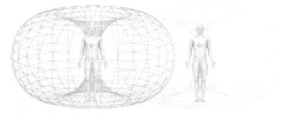

Magnetic Field of the Heart
Our thoughts and emotions affect the heart's magnetic field, which energetically affects those in our environment whether or not we are conscious of it.

Power of the Heart

The heart in all people radiates out a torus vortex that radiates around the whole body, as seen in a person's aura field. This aura field follows the same principles as discussed in how a torus vortex functions and how sacred geometry functions in earlier articles. The aura field around the whole body comes from the magnetic field of the heart. The higher the level of spiritual consciousness that someone projects out from their heart, the more energy their aura projects. This energy field around a person is the bubble around an enlightened higher frequency individual, seen in the many different Buddhist mandalas.

As you can see in the below image of the famous female Buddha Tara, like all the other enlightened Buddhas in the spiritual cannon, all high-frequency individuals have a circular aura field equal in dimension to the heart of the Buddha at the center of the aura field. The image below the title, "Painting of Buddhist Goddess Green Tara" by Prithvi Man Chitrakari in 1947, is another example of the energy emitted from the heart center (Wikipedia, 2011). In Buddhist mandalas, as far back as the earliest depictions of enlightened Buddhas go, it always shows that the most prominent human energy field around the Buddha's body always flows out from the heart. The higher the level of consciousness or enlightenment that a Buddha radiates at, the more brilliant the bubble or the Merkaba that the Buddha projects outward. As discussed in the previous subjects regarding the Merkaba and sacred geometry, the Flower of Life pattern is the two-dimensional pattern of the three-dimensional Sri Yantra, which is another form of seeing the scientific torus vortex, which is emitted out from the heart of every person.

A little background about the famous female Buddha Tara: she is a notable master teacher in Tibetan Buddhism. Tara comes in many forms to heal people, be compassionate to the suffering of sentient beings in their incarnation, and teach about nirvana's emptiness. Tara is revered for being the mother of all Buddhas and all Bodhisattvas. Much like the famous Bodhisattva, Kwan Yin, Tara too decided to come back to help people ascend into Buddhahood. *Tara is most notable for her life as a human who refused monks' recommendation during her lifetime to reincarnate as a man in the next lifetime. Tara clearly expressed that she will always incarnate as an enlightened woman. Anyone who sees hierarchy in gender is of lower consciousness because the one mind's universal energy sees no gender.*

Tara, female Buddha & Bodhisattva.
Advocate for female Buddhahood.

In investigating the heart's power as expressed in the stories about the female Buddhas, Kwan Yin and Tara understand that studying the mind is good. Living from within the heart is more powerful because it is not lost. It has always been right in front of mystics in Buddhist mandalas that show the heart's giant torus vortex. The Flower of Life is a pattern in sacred geometry. It shows that all sentient beings are connected through the unified field of consciousness because all living beings with a soul are a piece of divinity manifested.

This interconnection between people and the unified field of energy in the universe can be seen in the Global Coherence Monitoring System, which the Global Consciousness Project oversees. The Global Consciousness Project is a partnership with the HearthMath Institute, which conducts studies and lectures on the scientific findings, telling us that a person's heart is 5,000 times stronger than their brain. A person's heart sends out an electromagnetic pulse in every heartbeat. The hearth field is much larger than the field around the brain, as seen in Buddhist mandalas.

The emotions emitted from your heart can be felt within 5-feet away by the next person. You are having heart-to-heart communication with other people, which co-creates your collective physical experience.

Princeton University is recording the magnetic field of the Earth from different installations around the world. They look for spikes in their seismology equipment based on human beings' heart frequencies connected through the unified field as early indicators of anticipated events such as what happened in New York City on September 11, 2001. The event peaked at Princeton University's Global Coherence Monitoring System sensors four hours before it happened. This shows that people are connected, and we create our collective experience together based on what we believe and think spiritually.

Did you know that the health of our collective consciousness worldwide is being recorded every moment by the Global Consciousness Project at Princeton University? Whenever a major heartfelt event happens that affects many people's symbiotic hearts, such as Princess Diana's death, natural disasters, and the 9/11 terrorist attacks, the GCP generators record spikes in the Earth's magnetic field, which can be seen by space satellites.

Director of the Global Consciousness Project at Princeton University, Roger Nelson, Ph.D., published his research on the collective consciousness in the *Journal of Cosmology* in his article, "Detecting Mass Consciousness: Effects of Globally Shared Attention and Emotion". Roger Nelson explains that "A long-term research program called the Global Consciousness Project is designed to identify and study effects of mass consciousness engendered by shared attention and emotion. An operationally defined "global consciousness" appears to result from interactions of human beings around the world. We find statistical evidence for small effects from this source in the output of a network of devices that use quantum tunneling to generate random numbers. Detectable changes occur during great events of importance to humans, in which synchronized data collected at independent network nodes separated by thousands of kilometers become correlated. The correlations show that when the attention and emotions of large numbers of people are driven toward coherence by great tragedies or great celebrations, a small but detectable structure is imposed on our random data. The bottom line formal statistic shows a 6-sigma departure form expectations over the full 12-year database. This is evidence that human consciousness and emotion are part of the physical world, and the design of the experiment suggests a particular interpretation: we interact to produce a mass consciousness even though we are generally unaware that this is possible" (Nelson, 2011, p. 1).

The Global Consciousness Project researches collective consciousness and its effects on physical reality. The people living on Earth are unconsciously sensing ahead of the upcoming event, which occurs hours earlier. On August 7, 1998, the African Embassy Bombing was the 1st event that the Global Consciousness Project predicted with the science of random number generators in that area of the world. Since 1998, the Global Consciousness Project continues to collect real-time data on upcoming heartfelt events in different parts of the world. Time after time, the research data continues to predict the subsequent significant events based on the people's energy in that region.

In evaluating the methodology used by Roger Nelson, Ph.D., and his team at the Global Consciousness Project, physicist Peter Bancel, Ph.D. worked with Roger Nelson and his researchers' team for years. He evaluates if their method for calculating and understanding the information gathered from the different random number generators worldwide is sound. In the article, "The GCP Event Experiment: Design, Analytical Methods, Results," by Peter Bancel, Ph.D., and Roger Nelson, PhD., Peter Bancel wrote in detail the methods used by the Global Consciousness Project regarding their work with the random number generators are accurate. Peter Bancel worked with the team on many events and looked over the correlated data to conclude that the team is using sound scientific methods. His article shows that skeptics of consciousness research have little or no merit to back-up their cynicism regarding the study and frequently refuse to have an investigative approach to the data that continues to be indicators of collective consciousness as early predictors regarding upcoming events (Bancel, 2008).

The 9/11 terrorist attacks were the largest impactful heart-to-heart event recorded four hours before it happened by the Earth's sensors, which indicate that we are all intuitive but not all aware of it. Our planet is reacting to the collective broken hearts in each of us. To maintain a healthy world, we must keep a healthy heart full of unconditional love, forgiveness, and compassion for ourselves and each other.

In terms of measuring spikes in people worldwide's collective consciousness, the Global Consciousness Project has shown in over 20 years of researching heartfelt events in the Earth's Schumann frequency that every person living on planet Earth is connected. Everyone relies on the well-being of the Earth but is also connected to Earth themselves. Like animals in a herd, people become anxious and start retreating to safe areas to brace for an impending natural disaster unconsciously. People also react as a species to forthcoming events that they sense using their 6th senses. This heart-to-heart connection with the consciousness of the Earth shows that people are using their 6th senses regardless of conscious acknowledgment or not.

The GCP is an international, multidisciplinary collaboration that collects data through RNGs located in 70 host sites worldwide. They function as a seismograph during an earthquake but instead measures the collective consciousness of humanity worldwide as early warning systems for potentially affected areas that are the recipients of malicious human acts and natural disasters. The GCP was created to investigate quantum claims of collective consciousness in indigenous belief systems. Buddhism, Hinduism, shamanism, Native American traditions, Mayans, and so many more indigenous spiritual traditions believe that we live in a shared hologram with the Earth. Everything is mirroring projections of how we feel inside. We manifest it all together and individually. When a great event synchronizes millions of people's electromagnetic feelings from their hearts, a random number generator network becomes structured. The probability is less than one in a billion that the effect is due to chance. *In essence, we are connected through our hearts. When we hurt others, we hurt ourselves. We're all reflections of each other having different experiences. We need to learn to respect and love each other unconditionally as we are. We need to love and respect Earth every day!*

Notable examples of a heartfelt event predicted hours earlier through the seismology random number generators at over 70 locations worldwide are September 11, 2001, terrorist attacks on the NYC World Trade Center. The Global Consciousness Project (GCP) recorded a spike in the Earth's magnetic field many hours before the event occurred, which shows that we are one collective consciousness with Earth and that everyone is intuitive. During September 11, 2001, terrorist attacks at the U.S. World Trade Center, NASA satellites recorded a massive spike in the

Earth's magnetic field. They found it to be the cause because every person affected by the 9/11 attacks sent out a vast electromagnetic heart pulse, which was seen on the Earth's magnetic field from space. The Princeton random number generator was effected four hours before the attack, suggesting a worldwide collective intuition about the upcoming event (Global Consciousness Project, 2001).

Another example that spiked the random number generator in Pakistan can be seen in the Pakistani avalanche, which killed more than 150 soldiers on April 7, 2012. A massive wall of snow engulfed a Pakistani military complex close to the Siachen Glacier at 5:50 p.m. Rescue teams were unable to dig up any survivors. The missing soldiers are part of the Pakistani military deployment to the Siachen Glacier, which forms the northern part of the Kashmir region. This is a disputed region between Islamabad and India and the main source of tension between the nuclear-armed rivals who fought three wars since 1947. The GCP event was set for 6 hours, beginning at 9 a.m. local time (04:00 to 10:00 UTC) as an early indicator of an upcoming event, and was felt in the region's RNG. The result is 21765.623 on 21600 df, for p = 0.212 and Z = 0.798 (Global Consciousness Project, 2012).

In Somalia, the random number generators organized hours before the Mogadishu bombing on April 4, 2012, killing sports leaders. The Mogadishu bombing hit the capital of Somalia on April 4, 2012. Two of the country's most prominent leaders in sports were killed, along with eight others, and a large number of injured. The theater had only reopened its doors for the first time in 20 years in mid-March, an event which it hoped to marked a new chapter in Somalia's history. The GCP could not find the time of day for the bombing, but shadows in photos showed it was near noon. The GCP event was set for 12 to 18:00 local time (9 to 15:00 UTC). The result is Chisquare 22014.945 on

21600 df, for p = 0.023 and Z = 1.987 (Global Consciousness Project, 2012).

In California, the random number generators organized hours before the Oakland school shooting on April 2, 2012, which killed seven people. Around 10:30 a.m. a man who was named by police as a 43-year-old person opened fire in a classroom at Oikos University. It took the police officers hours to prepare to move the victims' bodies after a gunman killed seven people. The GCP event was set for 10:00 to 16:00, which includes 30 minutes before and several hours after the shooting began. The result is Chisquare 21462.563 on 21600 df, for p = 0.745 and Z = -0.659 (Global Consciousness Project, 2012).

In Honduras, the random number generators organized hours before the self-created Honduran prison fire on February 14, 2012, killing 358. A fire started by an inmate who tore through the prison Tuesday night, burning and suffocating screaming men in their locked cells as rescuers desperately searched for keys. Officials confirmed 358 dead, making it the world's deadliest prison fire in a century. Firefighters received a call at 10:59 p.m. local time. The rescue was marred by human error and conditions that made the prison ripe for catastrophe. The GCP event was set for 6 hours beginning at 11 p.m. local time in Honduras (05:00 - 11:00 UTC Feb. 15) as an early indicator of an upcoming event as felt in the region's RNG. The result is Chisquare 21757.060 on 21600.000 for p = 0.225 and Z = 0.757 (Global Consciousness Project, 2012).

The random number generators organized hours earlier in Colorado as the people of the area became unconsciously nervous. Shortly afterward, the Batman shooting that killed 14 people and injured 50 people on July 20, 2012, in Denver, Colorado, USA, occurred at 12:30 a.m. MDT. A gunman opened fire at a suburban Denver movie theatre on the opening night of the latest Batman movie, *The Dark Knight Rises*, killing 14 people and injuring at least 50 others. The GCP event was set for 6 hours, beginning at the shooting time, which was 12:30 a.m. local (06:30 UTC). The result is Chisquare 21932.562 on 21600.000, for p = 0.055 and Z = 1.595 (Global Consciousness Project, 2012).

In Wisconsin, the random number generators organized hours earlier to forecast the collective consciousness in that area was experiencing anxiety about an upcoming event soon to happen. Shortly afterward, the Sikh Temple Shooting occurred, killing six people and wounded others on August 5, 2012. In Oak Creek, Wisconsin, USA, a gunman opened fire at a Sikh temple near Milwaukee during morning service, and the suspected shooter later died in an exchange of gunfire with police. Six people were killed and others injured. The GCP event was set for 6 hours, beginning at 10:00 local time (15:00 UTC) and included minutes before the 911 calls, signaling the emergency. The result is Chisquare 21670 on 21600 df for p = 0.366 and Z = 0.341 (Global Consciousness Project, 2012).

In Syria, the random number generators of that area were organized because of the unconscious anxiety felt by the collective consciousness of the people living there on July 12, 2012. Shortly afterward, the Syrian Massacre, where over 350 people were killed in Tremseh, Syria, occurred. Yet, another massacre in the ongoing troubles in Syria took place in Tremseh. The attacks started apparently at 06:00 local time and continued for hours. The warring between the Syrian government and the rebel militia killed over 350 people in total. Tremseh is around 35km northwest of Hama. The GCP event was set for 6 hours, beginning at 06:00 local time. The result is Chisquare 21640 on 21600 df, for p = 0.422 and Z = 0.197 (Global Consciousness Project, 2012).

On July 27, 2012, in London, England, the random number generators in that area spiked before the Olympic Games Opening Ceremony. The

Opening Ceremony is a celebration showcasing the best of the host nation. It also features a parade of all competing nations and the highly anticipated entrance of the Olympic Flame, which ignites the cauldron and signals the games' start. The GCP event was set for 6 hours, beginning at 20:00 UTC, covering the full 5-hour ceremony plus an extra hour. The result is Chisquare 21542.527 on 21600 for $p = 0.608$ and $Z = -0.274$ (Global Consciousness Project, 2012).

Protest to Donald Trump's Muslim Ban on January 28, 2017, spiked the random number generators in the United States. The GCP event was set as the 24-hour day of January 28, UTC, which includes most of the huge buildup of protests at JFK and SFO, Dulles, O'hare, and many other airports. The result is Chisquare 87108 on 86400 df, for $p = 0.045$ and $Z = 1.699$. The chart shows an upward trend and hit a happy blue line. Earth was happy with this event where a huge collective of people expressed collective unrest for the unfair treatment of ethnic people affected by Donald Trump's Muslim Ban (Global Consciousness Project, 2017).

The Worldwide Women's March on January 21, 2017, also spiked the random number generators worldwide where these marches occurred. The GCP event was set for 12 hours from 7 a.m. to 7 p.m. Washington time. This period included most events in the United States and those in Europe, but probably not the earliest events in Australia and New Zealand. The result is Chisquare 43634 on 43201 df, for $p = 0.0705$ and $Z = 1.478$. This result is in accord with the Global Consciousness Project's prediction. The graph that was created out of the data collected from this day showed that the tendency for excess positive correlation is fairly persistent throughout the day. The chart showed an upward trend and hit a happy blue line. The Earth seemed to be happy with this event where mass amounts of people collectively voiced unity and support for female empowerment against the Trump administration in the United States (Global Consciousness Project, 2017).

The presidential inauguration ceremony of Donald J. Trump on January 20, 2017, spiked the random number generators in the D.C. area and many other RNG locations across the United States. The GCP event was set for 6 hours, beginning at 11:00 E.T. This included about 45 minutes of settling in. The ceremony itself started at about 11:50, with Donald J. Trump taking the Oath of Office administered by Chief Justice Roberts shortly after. The President then gave his Inauguration Address beginning at noon and lasting for about twenty minutes. There were several other presentations, invocations, music, poetry, and the ceremony ended around 12:30. The time of the oath is marked in the data. The graph created out of the data points that day showed a downward trend and did not even hit the happy blue line. Earth was not pleased with this event in the collective consciousness (Global Consciousness

Project, 2017). In twenty years of following spikes in this research, it seems that the Earth does not favor Donald J. Trump over other political leaders, which there appears to be no opinion. Some speculate that the Earth may be letting us know through her spikes in magnetic fields around the Trump administration that her environmental welfare could be harmed.

Ironically, the Farwell Address of President Barack Obama on January 10, 2017, also spiked the random number generators across the United States. This is a sharply focused event. Rather than the 6 hours typically analyzed, the Global Consciousness Project examined just two hours, from the beginning of the speech at 8 p.m. local Chicago time (02:00 to 04:00 UTC, on 11 Jan). The specified event includes much of the time Obama spent shaking hands and hugging supporters after his speech. The outcome is Chisquare 7217 on 7200 df, for $p = 0.441$ and $Z = 0.147$. What was seen in the graph created from the data collected is that there is no "Obama effect" like what was seen, which was measured as very positive by the Earth during President Barack Obama's presidential inauguration speech eight years earlier. The Earth and the population seem collectively happy to welcome in the Obama administration but were not happy to say goodbye to the Obama administration upon his farewell address. The chart collected showed a downward trend and did not hit the happy blue line that researchers look for in their evaluations. Earth and the majority of the collective consciousness of the western world were not happy with this event. The Obama administration was known to enact many environmentally friendly initiatives (Global Consciousness Project, 2017).

This research shows that the Earth has a consciousness, and she responds to the heart energy of the people living on her. However, Earth is the strongest magnetic and what she does to her own body affects every sentient being living on her.

When the magnetic field of Earth's Schumann frequency spikes, brace yourselves for something big because it affects everything on the planet. What this research found was that dense energy is brought up. In human history, this research found that when spikes happen, human renaissance occurs, and at the same time, human wars erupt. This is what is happening in the rising of the tides. If someone is of high caliber, they will experience a renaissance of abundance and creativity. If someone is of low consciousness, they will experience the rising of their inner havocs to resolve.

The heart's power is so much more magnanimous than any source of energy that the human body produces. Heart researchers found that by studying the long-term effects of heart transplant recipients, the original person whose heart the transplanted person receives it from continues to hold heart memory. Researchers of heart transplants found that the human heart has a tiny brain storing memories about the person born with that heart initially.

In the Mindshock Channel 4 documentary "Transplanting Memories?" heart transplant recipients report that the electromagnetic waves sent out from the transplanted heart manifest new experiences that correlate with the likes of the former person who owned that heart. In the documentary, heart transplant recipients reveal that they live out their heart transplant donors' preferences and memories, suggesting that heart research into memories held within the heart's tiny brain may be valid. Some notable examples are an 8-year old girl heart transplant recipient who helps police find and convict the murderer of her 10-year old murdered donor. Another noteworthy example among many in this documentary and many other reported heart transplant cases is a 47-year old Caucasian man who discovered a love for classical music and poetry after his heart transplant. The 17-year old African American girl who was this man's heart donor died from a drive-by shooting. She was a violin player and loved to write poetry.

Otherwise, transplanted patients of such unresolved heart memories will continue to play out such memories until resolved and synchronized with the new patients for a harmonious balance (Channel 4, 2006). Continued cases of heart transplants reporting new memories and preferences from their heart donors and learning to live with them are reported in the medical journals.

Profound medical discoveries are made into the heart's mind at the University of Montreal Center of Research and support by the Canadian Institutes of Health Research through John Andrew Armour, MD, Ph.D. Dr. Armour discussed in his article, "Little Brain of the Heart," published in the *Cleveland Clinic Journal of Medicine*, that the human heart has a nervous system made up of 40,000 neurons, which communicate with the human brain. This research shows that memories are not stored in the human brain but instead stored throughout the neural system (Armour, 2007). As cardiologists and medical researchers study the little brain in the heart, they found that the human heart works through a neural system that sends information to the brain.

The study of the human heart's magnetic power and the vast energy field around the person is used to create medical technology. Innovative Health Technology is a company that created the Biomeridian Testing machine. This machine measures the acupuncture points in the hands and feet that emit energy to measure the human energy field. Many ancient spiritual traditions consider the "human aura," or physics; they call it the "torus vortex." Many esoteric traditions believe that the human chakra system sends energy from the heart torus field into the torus fields of other chakras, which makes one big torus field around the body. This looks like a Buddhist mandala or, from the top view, a Yin Yang symbol.

The technology was a combined effort between Dr. Reckeweg and Dr. Reinhold. Dr. Reckeweg notably documented six phases of 600 different medical conditions. Dr. Reinhold confirmed the connection between the tissues and organs associated with varying acupuncture points in the human body. It is an excellent fusion between Eastern Acupuncture medicine and western medical research. The machine measures a patient's overall health based on their energy field (Biomeridian Testing, 2011). The Biomeridian Testing machine is a new medical technology that uses research about the heart's power and the human energy field around the heart to help people.

Buddhist monk, Barry Kerzin meditating with EEG for neuroscience and consciousness research.

Meditation Changes Reality

Neuroplasticity or brain research found that the brain also emits a smaller torus field, but not to the heart's magnitude. This has also been depicted for ages in many spiritual artworks worldwide, often accompanied by the human aura vortex. You're probably wondering what the big deal is about what brain researchers found regarding the profound implications of meditation? After a decade of studying how meditation practices change the world around them and increase the person's overall health conducting the meditation, brain researchers gathered so much evidence. Brain researchers confidently make the statement that meditation changes brain waves into Gamma waves. Those Gamma waves are a high level of brain wave frequency that emits energy from the person doing the meditation out into the field of our physical reality.

In short, meditation practices of any kind help change physical reality. The ancient Buddhist concepts about meditation transforming your physical reality into a new parallel reality, which matches your inner frequency, may be accurate. The Buddhist mandalas depicting a person in a meditation pose that carries them from one reality to another is actual. The only caveat is to know the validity of these personal shifts into new parallel realities, which can only be directly experienced. These residue experiences are what many mystics of Asia call "parallel realities" and what new age practitioners call "Mandela Effects."

To understand the value of meditation in your life, it is best to review scientific evidence. The distinction between prayer and meditation needs to be made. It helps us to realize how meditating in an empty state of awareness does change our physical reality. The value of prayer from the Buddhist perspective is that it is an act of "asking" the one mind of the universe for an outcome. Some examples of prayer are asking for financial assistance, asking for the welfare of a loved one in poor health, or asking for a variety of solutions to address an issue that someone is suffering with.

The ability to ask for a solution through prayer shows that someone acknowledges that they have a problem and is willing to entertain a proposed solution, which may answer that prayer. However, meditation is different because the person achieves a non-thought state of consciousness whereby the person has wholly emptied their mind and consciousness. The meditator has reached the emptiness of the mind, a blank slate. In this blank state of consciousness, it is someone making themselves open to receiving whatever the universal one-mind of the Lord wants to deliver. *It is the state of not asking anything to fulfill your physical reality but rather be open to what is received.*

According to many Eastern traditions such as Buddhism, when someone meditates and reaches the no-thought, empty state of consciousness, they can transcend reality by focusing on what is revealed. In Hindu, Buddhist, and Zen meditation practices, practitioners focus on the results because when you get in the empty state of consciousness, insert an image and feeling of whatever positive outcome you would like to experience. By doing so, you are changing your energy signature that emits outwards from your Merkaba. That energy signature affects the greater reality because reality is a construct reflecting the creator living it, the person, themselves. In eastern meditation practices, you are the great creator of your reality. Suppose you, as an energy being, decided to play in a collective reality. In that case, you, the creator, will intersect your Merkaba with others in the collective consciousness to create a new equilibrium reality.

When 1% of society performs transcendental meditation, they affect 99% of their community positively. Our individual and collective consciousness's effects are reprogrammed by large groups of people who meditate and collectively focus on the same outcome. The Alpha brain waves that they emit during meditation have been proven in numerous brain research studies to affect the unified field of universal consciousness, which changes physical and external reality. Transcendental meditation research is another way that explains how all people are connected through the unified field of consciousness and that the universal one-mind of the Lord resides in all sentient beings.

The Journal of Conflict Resolution published this article, "International Peace Project in the Middle East: The Effects of the Maharishi Technology of the Unified Field," in their December 1988 issue. The article outlines a 1968 study of the Maharishi Effect by Dr. Robert Keith Wallace at UCLA. When people focus on result feelings that an outcome has happened, not that it will happen, but that it's done. The societal outcomes reflect the electromagnetic energy sent out from the participants' hearts.

To prove this point accurate, over 60 scientific studies of meditation groups focus on peace in violent communities. In a case study, participants in war-torn areas of Israel and Lebanon were trained to feel the feelings of peace and oneness with the unified consciousness. It resulted in measurable results where terrorist activities drop to 0%, crimes declined, and hospital visits declined during the meditation time frame.

The mathematical formula that came from such experiments showed that only 1% of any population is needed to create the energy of positive, loving change in our collective holographic physical reality (Orme-Johnson, Alexander, Davies, Chandler and Larimore, 1988). The shift is you, the person meditating. People who practice meditation regularly through any form of activity that achieves that no-thought, Alpha brain frequency emits the frequency of change.

A collective consciousness emitting this frequency positively affects the unconscious collective, who for no reason known to them will behave slightly more peaceful during this time. The key for all practitioners of meditation is to live in a constant or almost constant state of Alpha brain waves so that their presence alone affects the greater reality wherever they are. These highly evolved people are walking beacons of positive energy affecting the field through their existence alone.

Decades later, the meditation research project that the Maharishi University of Management did continued its experimentation through the works of Quantum Physicist John Hagelin, Ph.D. John Hagelin, PhD. is the Director of the Institute of Science, Technology and Public Policy, International Director of the Global Union of Scientists for Peace, President of the United States Peace Government, Minister of Science and Technology of the Global Country of World Peace. In his published article, "The Power of the Collective" in the June-August 2007 edition of "Shift: At the Frontiers of Consciousness," Dr. Hagelin explains how in the summer of 1993, he organized a transcendental meditation group of up to 4,000 participants, and by the end of the meditation event which focused on well-being for the city of Washington, DC, USA, it worked. Historically, Washington, DC, has its highest crime rates during the summer months.

The meditation research group collaborated with the Washington, DC police department, the FBI, and 24 criminologists and social scientists from Temple University, the University of Texas, and the University of Maryland, to name a few. The results stated in the article documents, "We predicted a 20 percent drop in crime, and we achieved a 25 percent drop. In this case, it was only a few thousand people in a city of about a million and a half. So a relatively small group was influencing a much larger group. On days when the numbers of meditators were largest (and on a subsequent day), levels of conflict were remarkably reduced by about 80 perfect overall (Hagelin, 2007). Given the same experiment in transcendental meditation decades after the initial series of meditation research that the Maharishi Meditation Group did in the 1960s, John Haglin, Ph.D., and his meditation researchers got the same results.

Once a group of meditators reach non-local, empty consciousness through meditation and then focus their intention on a peaceful outcome for their city, the physical manifestation of Washington, DC was less violent by as much as 80% during that period. This shows that everyone lives in a holographic reality that manifests the level of consciousness and energy. The user who is self-aware and awakened during meditation creates their physical reality.

Since many souls are interconnecting their consciousness in a Vesica Piscis and Flower of Life pattern to be part of the same collective consciousness, then the small group of meditators who radiate at a much higher frequency changes the physical outcomes for Washington, DC. Meditation research shows that people can learn to emit higher personal frequency and change the dream for themselves. Together as a collective consciousness, change the collective holographic reality.

Eventually, many meditators can learn to achieve that state of consciousness all the time and change their external reality where ever they roam. The Buddhist distinction should be noted that the energy from such people affects the magnetics of the holographic reality that they exist in, but what is happening is a shift to a parallel reality where the positive outcome occurs. One cannot see the changes between parallel realities because the change occurs in an instant thought. The meditation event that was not positive exists in a lower, denser parallel reality to the Buddhist mystic.

It is essential to understand what a hertz is to understand brain frequencies and how they are measured. The hertz symbol "Hz" is a way to measure electromagnetic waves, as discovered by Heinrich Rudolf Hertz. Each hertz is one cycle per second. The more hertz, the higher the cycles per second of energy emitted outwards (Wikipedia, 2020). An easy way to understand this is if you take the analogy of shopping for a high-resolution television. A lower quality television will be lower hertz. This results in the cycles per second that each pixel displays, which shows how often the image refreshes. In short, a low-quality television has a picture quality of 60 Hz that will refresh 60 frames per second as compared to higher quality television, which refreshes 120 times per second or more.

The picture quality changes so quickly each second, and you cannot tell the subtle changes because the lag time between frames is so quick. The previous article about the collective consciousness and the Global Consciousness Project measures the Earth's heartbeat based on the electromagnetic waves in hertz that the Schuman Resonance picks up through seismology spikes. This functions much the same. The Earth itself has a consciousness, and it is raising its frequency through the Schumann Resonance. Every time the Schumann Resonance of the Earth spikes higher and higher up the hertz fields, it is refreshing its perceptual frames per second like a TV.

This was also covered in the Sri Yantra article, where I explain the Harmonic Voice Mandala as being each person, energy being in the form of a harmonic mandala or orb. A person's perception of self and reality is based on their level of consciousness or energy level, which receives the picture quality that matches their frequency. You may recall the earlier article on "Consciousness and Oneness," where I explain mental health doctor David R. Hawkins's work. He explained through his kinesiology work on calibrating the level of energy that a person of integrity and higher states of consciousness emit more energy into the field of reality around them.

According to the Map of Consciousness research, people who naturally emit high energy levels out of their aura fields (Merkaba) heal the world around them through their natural energetic state, which can be found in heightened states of consciousness during the practice of Zen meditation. According to a lifetime of research into consciousness that Dr. David R. Hawkins completed, higher frequency people offset many lower frequency people around them. This is precisely the conclusion from decades of meditation research. Those who exercise heightened states of meditation offset the greater reality of the unconscious population around them becoming more peaceful and harmonious.

Now that you understand how hertz measures the frames per second that reality is perceived through someone's consciousness level in their brain, you can get better familiar with different human brain waves and how it affects people. Although I compare brain waves to the hertz frequency of Earth's harmonic resonance when Earth's frequency hits a Gamma wave level hertz, the Gamma brain waves hertz in humans are not the same electromagnetic Gamma waves. It is an analogy to understand how energy is measured.

Brain wave researcher and author of the *Silva Method*, Jose Silva, explains the different brain waves. The highest level of hertz in the human brain is the Gamma brain wave (40-100+ Hz). The Gamma brain wave is often found in the meditation practices of monks and nuns. Feelings of bliss and gratitude induce Gamma brain waves, which exhibit a high level of consciousness and cognitive functioning that have been shown in Gamma meditation research to change reality. The following brain wave is Beta (14-40 Hz), which is a normal waking state and the level where your "ego" is most vital. Your "ego" is your persona outside of the collective consciousness of the universal one mind.

The next brain wave is Alpha (7-14 Hz), a relaxing state achieved during daydreaming or light meditation. In the Alpha brain wave, you can reprogram yourself for success. The next lower brain wave is Theta (4-7 Hz). Theta brain waves are attained through deep meditation and light sleep.

It's a level that connects you to the subconscious mind. Many meditators who reach this state talk about spiritual connectivity and oneness with the universe. The slowest brain wave is Delta (0,5-4 Hz), the level where awareness is fully detached (Silva,2009). All the brain waves are good states of being and have a purpose in our daily lives.

One notable brain wave for reprogramming your personal life that many meditators can achieve is the Alpha brain wave frequency. Again this frequency was shown in brain research to change the person's perception of self, and therefore the person can reprogram how they want to see themselves moving forward as they work to reach their success. In the 2009 edition of the *Journal of Alternative and Complementary Medicine*, the article, "Increased Theta and Alpha EEG Activity During Nondirective Meditation," explains that during extensive brain research into various meditation practices in a control group, many people were able to achieve Theta. Many often achieved Alpha brainwaves through meditation (Lagopoulos, Xu, Rasmussen, Vik, Malhi, Eliassen, Arntsen, Saether, Hollup, Holen, Davanger, and Ellingsen, 2009).

The article states, "Significantly increased *theta power* was found for the meditation condition when averaged across all brain regions. On closer examination, it was found that Theta was significantly greater in the frontal and temporal–central regions than the posterior region. There was also a significant increase in *Alpha power* in the meditation condition compared to the rest condition when averaged across all brain regions. It was found that Alpha was significantly greater in the posterior region than the frontal region" (Lagopoulos, Xu, Rasmussen, Vik, Malhi, Eliassen, Arntsen, Saether, Hollup, Holen, Davanger, and Ellingsen, 2009, p. 1).

Of the many brainwave frequencies that people emit throughout the day when practicing some meditation, they can quickly achieve the

Alpha frequency that gives them the ability to program their minds with the correct intentions they want to achieve a goal.

A popular technique that brain researchers found to help people in their overall health in psychology is to focus on forgiving others who caused pain in someone's life during the Alpha state of meditation. In the articles "Forgiveness and Alpha Waves" and "Doorway to Divinity at the BioCyberNaut Institute," Dr. James V. Hardt has a brainwave training facility in Canada. They help his clients learn to "forgive" and "let go" of repressed past issues with family, friends, and other love ones.

The meditative practice to reach Alpha and then focus on the act of forgiveness for personal well-being helps his clients reprogram themselves to stop the cycle of negative thinking, which they allowed themselves to be "conditioned" as being. Childhood conditioning in his clients causes a series of stress, anxiety, and depression-related medical diseases, which later show up in his client's overall physical health.

People can reach a non-thinking state of conscious awareness in Alpha using a variety of meditation techniques. Some modalities are lucid dreaming, yoga, making music, meditation, exercising, creating art, gardening, making a list of things to be grateful for, or any meditative practice that stops the musings of their everyday problems. The person in this state of Alpha can reprogram the holographic matrix they live on personally. Suppose anyone wants to have balance in their life. In that case, it is essential to connect to the universal consciousness through attaining the Alpha state in your brain waves to reprogram a new dream to be experienced and thus match a unique brain wave frequency that in synch with your new harmonious parallel reality (Hardt, 2012).

The research completed into the profound benefits of letting go of the anger that someone holds on childhood traumas through meditation in

Alpha brainwaves shows that the sage-old adage of forgiveness helps the afflicted person more.

Here is a Buddhist perspective regarding shutting down the loop cycle of thoughts in your mind to get into Alpha. One of the easiest ways to shut down the mind to prevent it from running thoughts in a loop cycle so you can get into the Alpha brain waves is simply the act of "acceptance." As Siddhartha Gautama taught, one of the Four Noble Truths is the teaching of letting go of one's "attachment" to those things, people, and illusions that cause suffering through the follow-up act of "acceptance." I outline the application of the Four Noble Truths extensively in my other book, *Buddhist Guide to Manifest Parallel Realties: Using the Four Noble Truths and Eightfold Path in the Age of Consciousness.*

In short, the Four Noble Truths are:
1. Life is Suffering
2. Attachment Causes Suffering
3. Insights Removes Suffering
4. Living the Eightfold Path Ends Suffering

The Eightfold Path is:
1. Correct Thought
2. Correct Speech
3. Correct Action
4. Correct Livelihood
5. Correct Understanding
6. Correct Effort
7. Correct Concentration
8. Correct Mindfulness

That's it. *Buddhism's primary tools in the Four Noble Truth and Eightfold Path can help someone change their perspective and actions. This changes their frequency, which shifts them into a new parallel reality.* Just accept everything as is. Could you stop trying to control it? Just accept. Once you say and are that, then the mind has nothing to think about over and over again. Acceptance is the stop loss and shuts down the factory of thoughts in mind. Accept all the drama that you dealt with by letting go of your attachment to it, and now focus on creating new experiences in Alpha so that you are alert to when the universe delivers the sequence of events that manifest your new experiences (Galt, 2016).

Once you achieve Alpha and start meditating on a new focus to reprogram your matrix to a parallel reality you want to be self-aware in, you will be better equipped in the 5th dimension. Everything you feel inside manifests faster. Time in the higher dimensions moves more quickly. Therefore, it is best to stop the mind's habit of focusing on the negative and your fears as that loop cycle will manifest. Your mind is not your enemy. It's one tool you have to help manifest your individual experiences aside from the collective experience.

Without the mind, all you have is the collective experience and not the individual experiences that enrich your spiritual growth. Your higher spirit in physical form allowed you to properly create beautiful experiences as reflections of your spiritual growth and be in tune with source energy's oneness is the leading-edge experience. If used properly, it is the best of the physical and the spirit world. So give your mind a break and use it properly to start manifesting consciously. Get into Alpha so you can manifest better, more loving experiences for yourself.

Many Buddhist meditation practitioners use the Hindu method of clearing one's mind to quickly get into an empty state of consciousness. That method focuses on your thoughts, which as a result, wipes clear your thoughts because the brain cannot think two thoughts simultaneously. Siddhartha Gautama founded Buddhism and carried over some of his Aryan family's Vedic Hindu traditions, which is why some Buddhist origins carry old Sanskrit Vedic insights into parallel realities based on the consciousness level of the spiritual mystic.

However, Buddhism has grown in its scholarly understanding of the nature of our holographic reality, parallel realities, the consciousness of self, the collective consciousness, and the unified consciousness with the universal one-mind since its inception in 500 BCE. Buddhism continues to evolve its approach to fact-finding research into its literary canon by eagerly incorporating active support and participation into the fields of consciousness, meditation, brain research, heart research, and the expanding fields of quantum-metaphysic study.

The basic premise for people who are new to Buddhism does not believe its findings are based on faith alone. The Buddhist philosophy requests its students to apply the knowledge into their own lives to have their own direct experience of parallel realities and become a master of their domain. At that point, you are equipped to teach others what you know most appropriately to you.

That little background into the meditation community's brain research may help you apply this Buddhist-Hindu meditation method. *Again, the sage-old technique is to focus on what your mind is thinking about at the moment. Since the mind cannot process two thoughts simultaneously, the brain will have a moment of the complete emptiness of any thoughts. When a meditator catches that moment of the void, hold on to it and if you are focusing on a specific outcome such as peace for yourself, then insert an image that resembles serenity to you. That is a simple Buddhist-Hindu meditation technique that anyone can achieve without much meditation experience, which will help you get into Alpha and maybe into the next highest level of brainwaves, Gamma waves.*

Alpha brainwaves are important in resetting your thoughts for a new you. However, in the 1980s, brain researchers discovered an even higher brain wave frequency called "Gamma brain waves."

In the study of meditation practitioners, brain researchers found that many experienced monks and nuns go beyond the Alpha brainwave and enter the Gamma brainwave frequency. To further understand how experienced meditation practitioners, which many monks and nuns regularly enter, brain researchers Claire Braboszcz, B. Rael Cahn, Jonathan Levy, Manuel Fernandez, and Arnaud Delorme conducted an extensive Gamma wave research study. They used three types of meditation practices often used by experienced monks and nuns in various Asian spiritual traditions. They applied an EEG brain monitoring system on different meditation groups from the Himalayan Yoga tradition, Vipassana tradition, and the Isha Yoga tradition. They instructed them to begin meditating using their modality of choice to 1. Meditate, and 2. Mind-Wander. Their collaborative research article, "Increased Gamma Brainwave Amplitude Compared to Control in Three Different Meditation

Traditions," was published by the University of Pecs Medical School in Hungary in the US National Library of Medicine National Institutes of Health.

Fig 1
The continuum of attentional engagement, from the high level of focused attention to more diffuse "open monitoring" or "open awareness" meditation.

The three meditation traditions we chose to include in our study can be placed along this continuum, each corresponding to a different focus of attention. Himalayan Yoga tradition uses a mantra to maintain the attentional focus, Vipassana tradition is primarily an open monitoring practice but the specific form assayed (as taught by S. N. Goenka) incorporates loose focus on the somatosensory awareness aspect and the Shoonya practice as taught in the Isha Yoga tradition is an open awareness meditation practice with no specific object to focus on

CCPL Source: US National Library of Medicine National Institutes of Health

The results from this study show scientific evidence that all meditation practices do reach Alpha states of consciousness, which explains how people can reprogram their intentions for their manifestations in that level of consciousness. However, the study went even further to show evidence that meditation practitioners have the ability with experience to achieve Gamma brainwaves. Gamma brain waves are the highest level of energy that a human brain can reach so far. Brain researchers know that Gamma brainwaves emit a frequency of 60 -110 Hz power. Research into experienced meditators who have vast experience working on developing their consciousness level is vital to brain research. It shows that these focused meditators with higher consciousness produce longer Gamma synchrony than regular meditation practitioners.

Summary of the main results.

	Himalayan Yoga	Isha Shoonya	Vipassana
Gamma power in MED and IMW	higher 60–110 Hz power than CTR group in MED and MED-IMW; trend for higher 60 –110 Hz power than CTR in IMW	higher 60–110 Hz power than CTR group in MED and MED-IMW; trend for higher 60 –110 Hz power than CTR in IMW	higher 60–110 Hz power than CTR group in MED and MED-IMW; trend for higher,60 –110 Hz power than CTR in IMW
Gamma in breath focus	lower 60–110 Hz power in MED than in breath focus	lower 60–110 Hz power in MED than in breath focus	no significant difference between MED and breath focus
Alpha	-	-	higher 7–11 Hz power during MED and IMW than all other groups

MED: Meditation
IMW: Instructed Mind-Wandering
CCPL Source: US National Library of Medicine National Institutes of Health

Gamma synchrony is the ability of meditators with higher consciousness to emit a much higher energy field into the environment, which an electroencephalograms (EEG) brain scanner can measure. The article "Zen Gamma" by David Dobbs in *Scientific American Mind Magazine* reports the brain research findings that the University of Wisconsin at Madison did with ten lifelong Buddhist monks and a group of student meditators. The EEG machine measured was that all Buddhist meditation participants reached high Gamma brainwaves for more extended periods than the control group of student meditators who also got Gamma brain waves. However, the student meditators' Gamma brain waves were not as high or lasted as long.

The article states that the result was, "More intense Gamma waves (30 to 60 or even 90 Hz) generally mark complex operations such as memory storage and sharp concentration. Gamma synchrony increases as a person concentrate or prepare to move. And lack of synchrony indicates discordant mental activity such as schizophrenia. Finally, a growing body of theory proposes that

Gamma synchrony helps to bind the brain's many sensory and cognitive operations into the miracle of consciousness" (Dobbs, 2005).

The Maharishi Meditation research studies and the many other universities continue to add more and more evidence to how meditation affects the consciousness of the meditators themselves and the unconsciousness of the mass population in the surrounding community where the meditation groups are practicing. Further brain research into consciousness and how our consciousness as an individual and as part of the collective consciousness have proven that reaching Gamma brainwaves is an example of high cognitive perception into our known reality.

The takeaway from this research into meditation is that everyone who practices regular meditation in any modality that suits them can reach Alpha brainwaves, which helps them reprogram their personal experiences based on the set of goals they have for themselves. Meditation research also shows medical evidence that everyone who meditates and builds up their consciousness level through inner spiritual work, such as many Buddhist monks, Buddhist nuns, and experienced meditation practitioners, does achieve a higher than Alpha brainwave. They reach Gamma brainwaves.

The EEG data shows that Gamma brainwaves are the highest energy that someone can emit outwards. Such individuals with higher levels of consciousness and energy affect 99% of the population around them positively. Therefore, meditation of any form is one of the best things you can do for yourself and the general public. Meditation allows people to tap into the universal mind's unified field and be awakened to the greater holographic reality in which all sentient beings exist. As such, those who are awakened spiritually, such as Buddhist monks and nuns for example, and working to increase their energy level up into Gamma brain waves and beyond are the awakened people who are changing the physical world around them to be more harmonious to nature.

Brain research shows us that 1% of the world's population is needed to change the holographic world we share as a collective consciousness. This is because these people change their frequency to match a higher parallel reality or create a new parallel reality that matches their energy level. Once created, other human energy orbs may choose to interact with them at that level instead. How much better would the world be if even more of the world's population practiced regular meditation and found a way to keep that energy level flowing daily?

Awakening & Ascension

To fully understand how to be a conscious manifester of parallel realities and explore parallel realities based on your everyday mundane decisions and the level of energy you emit from within yourself, one must experience a "spiritual awakening." A spiritual awakening is a phenomenon that can be studied and eventually achieved. Much like the phenomenon of being in love with a companion, it can be studied and observed. However, until one genuinely experiences the act of being in love, it is a mystery. *In Buddhism, a "spiritual awakening" realizes that they exist in a holographic reality that responds to the commands of its user.*

There is much scientific research into the phenomenon of spiritual awakening and what happens to your brain when someone has a spiritual awakening. Brain and psychology researcher Rick Hansen, Ph.D., Senior Fellow of the Greater Good Science Center at the University of California in Berkeley, and author of the best-selling book, *Buddha's Brain* explains what happens to a person working on attaining a Buddha brain neuroplasticity. In Dr. Rick Hansen's 2011 "Neurology of Awakening" lecture at the Wellspring Institute for Neuroscience and Contemplative Wisdom, he prefaces his lecture series, explaining the brain research into the scientific findings in evolved Buddhists that were part of such meditation research with this statement.

He says, "Buddhism is the contemporary wisdom I know best, and which has had the most cross over into western science probably because Buddhism shares two core values with western science. First, taking nothing on faith alone and then, second, pragmatism, a focus on causes and results. When you bring multiple traditions together, such as the western traditions of neural science and psychology, eastern traditions, and western religions such as Judaism, Christianity, and Islam, as well as others, you get cross validity checks. When the quantum physicists and the yogis point at the same moon, you get greater confidence and new methods. By studying the brain, we can get a better understanding of inner peace. We need to be open to new information" (Buddhas Brain, 2011). Brain research focuses much of its efforts on Buddhist brains. This is because test subjects of meditators, both experienced and inexperienced in various control groups of brain participants, produce the most profound results. Scientists found that the best EEG brain data comes from those participants who have a higher level of neuroplasticity and a higher level of energy emitting into the EEG machines in many Buddhist monks and nuns.

Frequently, they happen to be experienced Buddhist mystics. Hopefully, this will expand to all religious disciplines. Buddhism can act as a neutral bridge to a universal approach to consciousness while respecting your religious heritage. The best subjects with the most transparent and highest data happen to be highly evolved monks and nuns from Buddhism. However, various faith systems such as Hinduism and Christianity participated in the research and found remarkable neuroplasticity. In other words, spiritual mystics from all faiths who spent much of their life working on raising their consciousness level with unity to the unified field of the one universal mind emit Gamma waves into our holographic reality. Rick Hansen, Ph.D., explains that he found that *the brain functions much like a machine taking information from a person's nervous system in all the years of evaluating data from brain research. The nervous system is getting information that the brain is processing through subtle commands from the person's heart. Lastly, the person's nervous system that gets such information from the heart also gets comprehensive instructions from a non-local source entirely outside of the body. Profoundly, the human nervous system is getting information from the universal one-mind of all of consciousness and playing out the concept of individuality through the holographic expression of the person being studied in the EEG brain-machine.*

In Dr. Rick Hansen's 2011 "Neurology of Awakening" lecture, he states, "When you're thinking about the interaction with the mind and the brain. It's important to take into account long-standing religious and philosophical engagement. It immediately brings in questions about the spirit. The mind is the flow of information within the nervous system. The nervous system moves information around much like the heart moves, except the information is non-physical. Most of that information is forever outside of awareness. It consists of signals, learnings, inclinations, and expectations below the water line forever outside of consciousness. We privilege the tiny tip of the iceberg represented by the mental activity of the nervous system that we are aware of because it is what we know. *The brain's real action is in the underlying, semi-conscious habits of the heart for better or worse. All we know is what's in the frame of the mind. What you see right here is a fraction of what reality is without getting mystical. We see a very narrow band of the electromagnetic spectrum. We only hear a tiny range. A dog hears higher octaves. A hawk sees things we don't see. It's a constructed world. We live in a constructed world.* And yet, every event in the constructed world of conscious awareness maps one to one to an underlying neuro process. In the Hindu language, Nama is the world of consciousness. Rupa is the world of materiality. Every Nama has an invisible dance partner, an invisible Rupa. An invisible neurological event that co-arises with any mental event" (Buddhas Brain, 2011). Rick Hansen explains the industry's findings in compiling the brain research on control groups and groups of experienced meditators.

In the control group, brain researchers found that the brain's frontal cortex lights up in an MRI brain scan when someone feels rewarded, such as cocaine users and someone who wins the lottery. These same addictive reward sensors in the brain light up in a boy who sees his girlfriend's images or a Tibetan monk who focuses on compassion for all sentient beings. In another study of female nuns from a Christian monastery who was hooked up to MRI scans and asked to focus on profound spiritual experiences, even more areas of the reward centers lit up. This evidence shows that the more inner spiritual work someone does on themselves, the more compassionate and empathetic they become to others. This is a result of twisted strands of DNA in the brain unpacking more atoms. The neurology of an awakened person's brain shows that regular meditation exercises the cortical tissues in the brain's frontal lobe, which results in a denser brain and slows the aging process. DNA degeneration through aging happens when long telomeres at the end of DNA chromosome cells shorten over time.

Red blood cells die every minute in the body, and new red blood cells are being copied every minute, and the longer the telomeres on the end of your DNA chromosomes, the better the new cells. Regular meditation exercises your red blood cells and keeps them healthy, according to brain research. Telomeres on the end of chromosomes protect that chromosome from fusion with other chromosomes or decay. Brain research also shows evidence that pain and helplessness are easy to learn. The brain will lock in negativity to remember it more than positive daily experiences because it is a survival mechanism to teach people through muscle memory what hurts them and avoid it.

However, someone who submits to repetitive patterns of anger, resentment, blame, and self-hatred causes their brain to decay faster. Compared to someone who focuses on positive experiences of compassion, kindness, and gratitude, it produces a more potent, denser, healthier brain and can deal with challenges faster and better. *Research into this learning mechanism to latch onto negativity that decays the brain compared to focusing and building on positive experiences in everyday mundane activities was conducted on dogs who felt the pain of an electric fence. Researchers had to drag dogs that were kicking and whimpering over to the invisible fence and lifting them over the fence to show them how to overcome this problem. Ironically, many people's brains are much like dogs in this study concerning painful experiences as teaching moments for many people. It seems that researchers may have to exhaust themselves with positive solutions to get people who are stuck on painful memories to challenge their fears and cross over.* The takeaway of "Buddha's Brain" from bringing forth the brain research findings is that everyone can have an awakened brain's neuroplasticity through meditation (Buddha's Brain, 2011). The comparison can be made to explain how so many people do not enact positive solutions that better their overall livelihood because, much like how dog's brains work, they learn through painful lessons that have muscle memory.

Non-violent spiritual friend and mentor to the late Martin Luther King Jr. Buddhist Zen monk Thich Nhat Hanh gave a 2006 lecture to the United Nations Educational, Scientific and Cultural Organization (UNESCO). He stressed the world's importance to have a collective awakening into unity consciousness out of the ego's desire for separation. The lecture "A Collective Awakening for the Future of Our Planet" by Thich Nhat Hanh speaks about the Buddhist tradition of a personal awakening or enlightenment, which is one pathway out of many that can lead towards spiritual growth. It's critical now to have a planetary collective awakening worldwide as the illusion of separateness from long misinterpreted or manipulated ideologies lead us towards extinction.

Humanity is in a race to turn the tides into a safer harbor. It is essential to have a collective awakening before our destruction of the planet. Earth makes our home planet no longer hospitable to all sentient beings living on it. We need to create systems of commerce that live symbiotically with Earth. The Earth needs good stewards and caregivers of all kinds. Such a call requires a worldwide business to create a livelihood that offers people careers to make a good living caring for the environment. Humanity is an expression of the universal one mind, and Thich Nhat Hanh believes people can transform into a galactic society worthy of interstellar commerce and cultural exchange.

We will destroy ourselves if we don't unify much of the cells of our human body. The most common thing in our way from balancing and peace in our inner being is our ego. Your ego is a tool of your body to have an individual experience aside from the collective experience. Give your ego a break. It was not designed to do the hard work of manifestation, as it will likely create negative situations as it is out of balance with your heart and not in unity with universal consciousness. Your higher spirit has a human experience. Therefore, your soul knows the fastest and most harmonious way to manifest by directing your ego and mind to use the largest organ in your body; your heart. A balanced life will have harmony with your mind, body, and spirit. In the Plum Village monastery in France, where Thich Nhat Hanh resides with lay practitioners, monks, and nuns, they display examples of how over 10,000 public attendees can be peaceful in their everyday mundane activities. The everyday beingness of having a peaceful nature can be experienced in mindful walking meditation, mindful breathing, active listening, and various gentle ways to live. It will foster personal awakening to our unified consciousness's great reality and bring about a more peaceful world with less suffering. This call is not religious but universal (Hanh, 2006).

All spiritual awakenings lead to the conclusion of what Consciousness Studies found: all people are part of one significant unified consciousness. All religions and all science point to the same conclusion: "consciousness" is the basis of everything in existence. Everyone and everything in existence plays out its part in a holographic game for the universal one-mind of consciousness to experience itself.

Everything physical is energy in form, which is a creation out of the mind of the individual's consciousness and the collective consciousness of the whole. It is all playing out for the self-realization of the unified field of energy in the universe. To understand this quantum view of consciousness, God, Allah, or whatever name people label the universal consciousness in all people as, quantum physicist and author Amit Goswami, Ph.D. do an excellent job explaining his findings from his lifetime of research into this field of study. After retiring as a Physics professor at the University of Oregon (1968-1997), Amit Goswami, Ph.D., published over 15 books on consciousness research and how consciousness creates the matrix. Dr. Amit Goswami's most popular books are *The Self-Aware Universe*, *Physics of the Soul*, and *How Quantum Activism Can Save Civilization: A Few People Can Change Human Evolution*.

Dr. Amit Goswami explains in his interview, "A Quantum View of God" with Mel Van Dusen, that fundamental, religious views of God have kept many people held back in their spiritual growth. The research into quantum physics and the flow of energy between people meditating proves that non-local energy flows through all people since we are all interconnected beings to the same non-local consciousness. Duplicate research was completed by the University of Mexico and many other universities. The research subjects were told to meditate for twenty minutes and focus on non-local consciousness. Then they are separated, and one meditator is shown a series of flashes.

The EEG brain scans of both participants found that the other meditator who was separated in a completely different room experiences the same energy that flows through their brain scans. It is as if this participant who is not shown the flashes of light is behaving just like the other meditator exposed to the flashes of light. This is much like the research into the heart's power, where someone's heart cannot tell the difference between painful experiences happening to themselves or another person (Van Dusen, 2008). In the interview "A Quantum View of God", Dr. Goswami states, "Quantum activism is activism which helps us to change ourselves and our society using the basic principles of Quantum Physics. What are some of these basic principles? One principle is non-locality. *Non-locality is signal less communication. The idea that we share a non-local consciousness. Consciousness is the same for all of us. It's cosmic consciousness. This cosmic nature of consciousness implies that I must be good to my fellow sentient beings because we are one at some non-ordinary state of consciousness. We are one. You and I are not separate after all. Therefore, your goodwill does me good also. These ethics are burned into quantum thinking and cannot be excluded from the way we live. This is one example of how quantum principles enable us to re-establish living within values and virtues* (Van Dusen, 2008). Working to achieve inner balance energy by being the embodiment of such quantum ethics is another way to ascend your consciousness level. All living beings such as humans share the same non-local consciousness, acknowledged by many indigenous cultures and mystic spiritual traditions. All people, regardless of the conditioned hierarchy, have the opportunity to choose alternate parallel realities to experience through the consciousness of the universal non-local one mind.

In Buddhism, the basic concept of "ascension" is to raise your energetic frequency by living the best version of you as embodied in the positive and abundant aspects of the universal one mind. As a result of being the highest version of yourself that you can radiate at, you become a gift to the universal one-mind. The union of consciousness with the self and the universal self results in positively affecting those around you. It happens through the energy that your level of consciousness emits outwards into the matrix of reality in which matter is created. In Buddhism and the Vedas of Hinduism, it is taught that your inner radiance manifests a parallel reality that matches the internal frequency you emit. Simple physics of like matching like in terms of energy. There are no judgments. No one makes any judgments on which reality you experience next. It is a simple act of energy organizing itself to the most harmonious frequency to whatever sound you are beaming at the time.

In the earlier article on the Map of Consciousness by David R. Hawkins, MD, Ph.D. as written in his 2005 book *Truth Vs. Falsehood: How to Tell the Difference*, you may recall that he spent his life work on mental health. He discovered that everyone has a certain level of consciousness towards enlightenment between 0 – 1,000 based on the inner characteristics that they embody. According to Dr. Hawkin's kinesiology research, while he was alive, there are currently only 15% - 20% of society with integrity who measures at the acceptable minimum 200 on the Map of

Consciousness. This is the fundamental benchmark to be an excellent barometer to conduct kinesiology questioning on. The rest of society is working to reach 200 in terms of their level of energy. Often, Dr. Hawkins compared his people's calibrations to their contributions to the community and how they lived their lives.

Politicians, business owners, and various people in our society show by example that they behave at the calibrated level that the Map of Consciousness measures them at. When tested under challenging situations, someone who calibrates at below 200 often does not have the integrity needed to care for others' well-being. Often, these people struggling with their narcissism and need to survive at the cost of others. They are walking life lessons. Since much of the world is not aware of measuring people's energy, they get blindsided by the facade and vote in megalomaniacs.

Map of Consciousness Scale

700 – 1000	Enlightenment
600	Peace
540	Joy
500	Love
400	Reason
350	Acceptance
310	Willingness
350	Neutrality
200	Courage
175	Pride
150	Anger
125	Desire
100	Fear
75	Grief
50	Apathy
30	Guilt
20	Shame

His kinesiology muscle testing research shows that everyone is connected in terms of the same non-local universal consciousness. Everyone can attain higher levels of energy in their inner spiritual work towards achieving enlightenment at some point in their soul's physical incarnation (Hawkins, 2005). Much like the basic principles of Quantum Physics and Consciousness research have done in academia. Many of the world's most popular religions currently focus on fostering the characteristics of the lower half of the Map of Consciousness. The lower characteristics of scientific research into meditation, heart power, and brainpower do not match Gamma brain waves' higher frequencies, which directly connect to the universal one-mind in all sentient beings.

The attributes of self-aware people enough to realize shifts in parallel realities often match the characteristics in the top half of Dr. David R. Hawkins Map of Consciousness. As in the discussion in the previous article, "Meditation Changes Reality" in this book, the human brain naturally gravitates to painful and fear-based experiences as a survival mechanism. The muscle memory of painful experiences helps prevent repeating the same mistake compared to focusing on positive experiences that scientifically prove to keep neuroplasticity in the brain and nervous system healthier and aging gracefully. The challenge for the human nervous system and brain is to focus on the positive aspects of their spiritual cannons, which are the building blocks of their belief systems that make up how they see the world and the people around them.

In Buddhism, monks and nuns do much to use Gamma wave meditation to locate their next lama leader and Tulku children. They incarnate into our physical world to help their brethren carry on their spiritual legacy. There is no politics or lineage involved in who becomes the next Dalai Lama. For example, Buddhist monks and nuns have for thousands of years geo-located the person with the highest level of energy and a spirited match to the specific sound DNA signature of their spiritual leader's previous incarnation using Gamma brainwave meditation. As you may recall in the earlier chapters on sacred geometry, every person on Earth has a unique sacred geometric shape or personal mandala unique to them. Higher evolved beings make decisions based on which choice is radiating at a higher frequency.

The pathway to having a personal awakening is introduced, and the path towards ascension into higher levels of consciousness has been explained. You are ready to explore parallel realities through consciousness, much like many Buddhist mandala depictions of enlightened Buddhist teachers, exploring parallel realities. Many notable Buddhas, such as the female Buddha from China, Kwan Yin, as depicted in this book cover, are often depicted in Buddhist mandala artwork as someone who decided to do Bodhisattva service to humanity. She teaches the principles of consciousness that reach enlightenment, and by doing so, she helps raise the level of consciousness of her students in whatever parallel reality she pops into. A Bodhisattva in Buddhism is a soul that chooses to hold off on letting go of their ego to walk through the final doorway and become reabsorbed into the pure energy of the universal one mind. Instead, she decides to do service to humanity by helping all sentient beings reach enlightenment. In his book, *Power vs. Force*, Dr. David R. Hawkins discusses that he remembers being happy as part of the void of spiritual emptiness and beyond. He had no intention of reincarnating. However, he was sucked out of that existence to be a human boy. At that moment, he recalls walking out of a drowning incident to do his service to humanity at this time. His service mission was to help raise consciousness by contributing his dharma wisdom before departure.

British Author of Buddhism, Taoism, and Zen traditions, Alan Watts, said this about the Bodhisattva journey for an enlightened being who knows the game of consciousness, which many people are unaware of playing. Alan Watts states, *"There are two kinds of Buddhas. The Pratyeka Buddha is a private Buddha who doesn't tell anything, or you can become a Bodhisattva.*

*Pratyeka Buddha goes off into his ecstasy and never is seen again. Bodhisattva comes back and appears in the everyday world and plays the games of the everyday world by the rules of the everyday world, but he brings with him Upaya, some way of showing that he's been on the journey, that's he's come back, and he's going to let you in on the **secret** too. If you will play it cool and also come back to join in everyday life of everyday people."* This topic of Bodhisattvahood is debated among many Buddhist traditions as it is a personal choice, and either option is acceptable in the direct experience of the universal one-mind who is experiencing the ecstasy of either choice directly. Science proved with the double slit experiment that two atoms can be at the same place simultaneously and still communicate with one another. Therefore, an advanced soul can be a Buddha and a Boddhisatva at the same time. Since everything exists in the present, all of existence are parallel realities.

Many traditions talk about parallel realities, but many spiritual and religious traditions use different terms to explore other realities. Regardless of the terminology used, such as personal choices, pathways, roads, I AM, the law of attraction, the law of intention, or any other concepts for manifesting from within yourselves an experience different from what was previously experienced, it is all talking about the nature of reality.

In Buddhism, it is clear, all experiences are parallel realities, and everyone is experiencing the reality that matches their frequency. Everyone is getting the lessons in the parallel reality that fits them. If you see suffering directly, send love and hope so that they may overcome their hardships. The perception that someone holds about the nature of their current reality dictates their next parallel reality with all the parallel versions of that next experience. The level of someone's awakening and ascension dictates how much of their parallel reality they will consciously experience.

It's proven in science that there are parallel realities that all exist at the same time with parallel people, parallel events, varying histories, and parallel things. In the article "Multiverse" by author Caillo Loken, he writes about the 1979 Nobel Prize Winner in Physics, Steven Weinberg, who supported the concept of Multiverses when he said, "There are hundreds of different radio waves being broadcast all around you from distant stations. However, if you turn on a radio, you can listen to only one frequency at a time; these other frequencies are not in phase with each other. Each station has a different frequency, different energy. As a result, your radio can only be turned to one broadcast at a time. Likewise, in our universe, we are tuned into the frequency that corresponds to physical reality. But there is an infinite number of parallel realities coexisting with us in the same room, although we cannot tune into them." This understanding of varying radio waves and frequencies to distinguish between varying parallel realities is accepted in the scientific community.

Various Consciousness research disciplines show that all people have different energy signatures based on their level of consciousness. We also know from kinesiology research from David R. Hawkins, MD, Ph.D. that other countries and cities also have their energy level on the Map of Consciousness scale. Therefore, each reality's concept as a location in the universe has its energy signature, just like each location on the Earth has its latitude and longitude. If someone wants to travel and explore different physical locations on Earth, they need to travel to that latitude and longitude on Earth. This is the same concept that many Physicists understand, which is specific frequencies structure those parallel realities. People can explore those frequencies base on matching their energy signature through their level of energetic consciousness. This is a concept that many Physicists theorize on how portals may build emerging technology in our near future.

People are made of atoms. Atoms are held together with energy. The legendary double-slit experiment done by British Scientist Thomas Young in 1801 was one of the earliest demonstrations of Physics that showed how the wave of light behaved. Thomas Young directed a beam of light towards two equally separate slits. The same beam of light became two different but identical waves existing in two separate locations. The two identical waves of light eventually reunited as one. The double-slit experiment in Physics proved to the academic community that light is both waves and particles. This evidence shows how atoms and molecules behave the same. Western Electric company researchers Clinton Davisson and Lester Germer conducted duplicate experiments to scatter electrons on a crystal on a nickel-metal surface. They found that it behaves the same way (Wikipedia, 2020). The double-slit experiment has been repeated thousands of times at various universities and research labs, and the data is the same. *Two atoms can exist in two completely separate spaces as the same atoms and still communicate with one another in some subtle way. Scientists are still trying to figure out to reunite as one being eventually.*

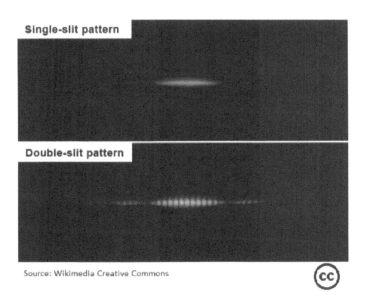

Source: Wikimedia Creative Commons

It is proposed by Buddhist and Hindu teachings that humans are made up of the same material of light and energy, and as such, do exist in multiple parallel realities simultaneously. The only way for people who know if they are experiencing a parallel reality is if their current reality has physical elements that they do not previously remember. Parallel realities and parallel people are a twilight zone phenomenon that can only be experienced. Evidence of parallel realities may be substantiated by backed-up memory of the same history from other people in a modern phenomenon called "the Mandela Effect."

The Mandela Effect is a phenomenon where many people recall two different outcomes for the South African politician, Nelson Mandela. Large groups of people remember that Nelson Mandela died in prison, and other large groups of people recalled that Nelson Mandela died years after he became president of South Africa. It is debated how such large numbers of people identify two different versions of reality. This is one of many Mandela Effect phenomena. In Buddhism and Hinduism, Mandela Effects are simple examples of exploring parallel realities by changing your energetic frequency through your consciousness level by being a conscious tourist who travels between parallel worlds.

Another compelling evidence about parallel realities comes from the vast investments in the quantum computer. The humble beginnings of the D-Wave Quantum Computing Company began as an offshoot of the Department of Physics and Astronomy from the University of British Columbia in Canada through university students and professors Haig Farris, Geordie Rose, Bob Wiens, and Alexandre Zagoskin. The early research collaborated with a vast array of scientists from the Leibniz Institute of Photonic Technology, Université de Sherbrooke, University of Toronto, University of Twente, Chalmers University of Technology,

University of Erlangen, and Jet Propulsion Laboratory.

The D-Wave Quantum computer is profound evidence to support the science behind parallel realities because of its design. A regular computer functions in "bits", which allows it to read computer code in "1" and "0", one at a time. A quantum computer's processor runs in "qubits," which, much like the double-slit phenomenon in Physics, works using "superposition." Superposition in quantum computers allows the processor to superimpose 1s and 0s at the same time. What results is a computer where the user asks the quantum computer a question. The answer from the internet in that computer provides solutions that do not exist in our current reality. This implies that a quantum computer is tapping into the parallel internet network that exists in parallel realities. Since the World Wide Web is energy signals not held to physical rules of matter, a quantum computer can tap into all the parallel internet signals to get answers to complex questions. Since beta testing this to interested investors, initial purchasers were Lockheed Martin, the University of Southern California, Google, NASA, and Los Alamos National Lab (Wikipedia, 2020). Since the launch of an experimental prototype, quantum computer technology has exploded in investor funding.

Many investors are interested in using quantum computers to explore ideas to check the feasibility of projects before investing lots of money into an idea that may or may not work. As the bridge between science and metaphysics merge, I fully expect to see even more evidence of parallel reality discoveries. Hopefully, knowledge of parallel realities and how things transpired in other realities becomes a learning lesson for people to live more symbiotically with Earth.

Conclusion

"The planet does not need more successful people. The planet desperately needs more peacemakers, healers, restorers, storytellers, and lovers of all kinds."
–Tenzin Gyatso, 14th Dalai Lama

I did not intend to have a public profile at all. I have a peaceful life ahead of me, and I want to keep it that way. I was never interested in challenging my consciousness with spiritual narcissism, which brings down my energy field. However, in 2011-2012, there was so much paranoia regarding the Mayan calendar. Much of that paranoia was displayed in the west due to fears of religious Armageddon. In the eastern part of the world and to many indigenous cultures worldwide, the year 2012 is believed as the end of the cycle of separation. We welcomed the next phase of humanity into a new cycle of unity and cooperation. We crossed the threshold into our galactic golden age of consciousness. How fast humanity transitions into this era with planet Earth is up to humanity itself. Earth and that 1% of higher frequency people are already migrating to the higher levels of existence. The storm is pulling everyone else at whatever level they are at. All their dense issues are pulled up with them to resolve or fall back to a lower dimension to carry on their lessons in the parallel reality that matches their energy level.

Currently, there is not much evidence to prove that the Buddhist folklore about an ancient Lemurian civilization in the Pacific Ocean ever existed. Many indigenous tribes and traditions such as Buddhism keep the knowledge about the upcoming end of this cycle of separation in humanity. While the west retreated into paranoia about the end of the world according to their religious beliefs, indigenous tribes like various Native American elders, Mayan elders, Polynesian chiefs, and many Buddhist monasteries ushered in the new cycle of unity consciousness with awakening ceremonies around 2012 AD.

In Buddhism, the tradition begins the dating system differently than the Gregorian dating system. The year 2012 BCE in Buddhism is dated as the year 2,555 BE (Buddhist Era). The 2,555 is a year of changes and was seen as a cosmic joke year, which many eastern countries saw. The cultures that did not maintain their ancient tribal knowledge from long ago lost insight into the global awakening of 2012. They missed being part of the Awakening ceremonies.

Buddhism is an ancient spiritual approach to the nature of our holographic existence that sprang from offering free scholarly education to patrons. Over time, studying various medicine, astrology, cosmology, literature, and all areas of metaphysic exploration turned into monastic life. Buddhist monastic institutions became community outlets for solace in providing food and support to the monks as they became scribes of written knowledge. Some of the written literature in Buddhism documents local history, such as the megaflood that wiped out ancient Lemuria and other ancient advance human civilizations of the past. Over thousands of years, local oral history became Buddhist legends.

Just like all tall tales and legends told in the Buddhist canon about the nature of our holographic reality and how to navigate it, I listened and was very entertained as a child. Like many other religions, Buddhist literature had suitable lessons and cautionary tales to live life as best as one can with what they are working with. I was only interested in the master teachers and how they could quickly shift between different parallel realities. All the Buddhist mandalas in all the Buddhist literature I ever read are consistent. Men and women who are awakened and ascend their energy fields become conscious beings in the world. Through their consciousness, men and women shift between different parallel realities based on their mandala's energy level. So I kept my knowledge of Buddhist mandalas and waited and waited to see if it was true or if they are fable.

In college, which is 20 years ago for me, I started to follow many Buddhist monks, Buddhist nuns, and the Dalai Lama who actively participate with academia to study the nature of Meditation, Quantum Physics, and Consciousness Studies. All the different studies I came across in academia on various aspects of sacred geometry and consciousness piqued my attention. Year after year, and research paper after research paper, I followed many academic fringe researchers' life work into various areas of metaphysics, mindfulness, consciousness, and anything pseudo-science. Because of the tremendous independent fascination of many pseudo-science researchers into these topics, I was able to piece together all the scientific research to back up my lifelong understanding of Buddhist mandalas. I hope I did a fair job explaining their collaborative efforts in raising human consciousness towards our next-level existence in a shared hologram.

I kept my knowledge to myself and did not reveal much of it to others because people are allowed to explore parallel realities anyway they like. They will experience the reality that is a fit for them and grow from those experiences in their life. However, after speaking to the monks at my mother's temple about the 2012 paranoia some people had, they advised me that it is wise to share my Buddhist perspective and metaphysical knowledge to reduce their suffering. So, I regretfully did. My boyfriend at the time, who is now my husband, helped me deflect all the anger from people calling me names and insults for sharing my Buddhist knowledge on social media because it challenged their belief system.

Over sixty metaphysical post articles regarding unity consciousness in sacred geometry are seen in the spiritual awakening process in Buddhism and many other indigenous traditions worldwide in my personal Facebook timeline photo album from 2011-2012. Each post article has pictures that explain the logic and is backed up with scientific evidence that I gathered at the time. Some people can be so mean and demeaning because the scientific evidence I gathered challenged their limited worldview.

I kept telling people who tried so hard to convert me to their religion that there is no point in converting a true Buddhist because we are all incarnated on Earth to play this big game to learn and grow from the Earth experience. If we choose to reincarnate again, we hopefully would have ascended to a higher level of consciousness to access incarnating into lifetimes in other games in the galaxies, parallel realities, and dimensions. I tried to explain Buddhist mandalas, awakening, ascension, and shifting to better and better parallel realities based on changing your perspective in your consciousness on any subject you are working on. Many of it fell on deaf ears because Buddhist mandalas are something that has to be directly experienced.

We can take action towards that intention using the Buddhist Four Noble Truths and Eightfold Path, which is one strategy among so many more Buddhist strategies for shifting your consciousness's trajectory from one perspective to another. By doing so, you change into a parallel reality that matches that new resonance you are now emitting. It was all too fantastic, and many people's eyes glazed over. So I waited and waited and continued to learn about sacred geometry, metaphysics in academia, and independent fringe research.

I tested my sacred geometry and consciousness material on my personal Facebook page, which showed me that being exposed to this content does help people become spiritually awakened and encourages readers to begin pursuing their ascension process to perfect their energetic mandala. I infused a lot of research to show that the message of awakening and ascension through sacred geometry is also seen in many spiritual traditions outside of my Buddhist understanding.

I've seen similar references to awakening and ascension through sacred geometry in Celtic, Native American, ancient Hindu, ancient Egyptian, Mayan, and in artwork from temples even older than Egyptian artwork going further back beyond the Indus Valley civilizations over 13,000 years ago before the megaflood. Sacred geometry artwork in temples goes so far back in ancient times that no one today knows how old these temples are. I would not even be surprised if nautical archaeologists discover ancient temples in deep oceans not far from various coastlines worldwide and discover many of them have similar sacred geometry and metaphysic decorations.

This book is the product of my lifelong fascination with Buddhist mandalas. What began as social media blog articles to help alleviate suffering from the 2012 end of the world paranoia that some people experienced turned into enough research to compile into a three-book set. This book is the first of three books. This book gives you a basic understanding of how sacred geometry in all religions and spiritual traditions worldwide is all the same. I use 20 years of scientific research to prove that Buddhist mandalas are an ancient understanding of how to exist in our holographic world.

The takeaway from all this scientific research in sacred geometry seen in Buddhist mandalas is that everyone incarnated on Earth has a human experience in this holographic game of life. Everyone was equally born into a human lifetime for various reasons to learn, grow, and ultimately experience what life is like as a human on Earth. It is a complex fabric that is weaved into why people have so many different human experiences, but it is experienced 1st hand.

The most courageous souls choose this incarnation on Earth because there is no manual for awakening our physical reality's holographic nature. There is also no manual for raising your energy level to the higher states of consciousness. Lastly, there is no manual to realize that you are existing in a Merkabah that is carrying you from one parallel reality to another based on the energy level you emit from your consciousness. The only inclination that many people have about how powerful they are as creators of our holographic world is seeing slight variations to their current existence that they remember differently from before they changed their perspective on something that changed their energy level.

Studying sacred geometry in Buddhist mandalas tells us that all religions have master teachers who travel between parallel realities in a large Merkabah. These master teachers in Buddhism are called "Buddhas." They're regular people who awakened to the more fantastic game. These master teachers in all our world religions shift their energy to match the parallel reality that matches their energy level. There are Buddhas in all dimensions, all parallel realities, and all places in creation, as seen in this book's various Buddhist mandala artwork.

Buddhas can return home to the void for infinity by letting go of their addiction to continue to experience the fullness of creation as an individual being separate from the wholeness of the universal one mind. Some may even pop out of the void to help relieve the suffering of humanity further out of ignorance and into higher levels of consciousness so that they too can journey reality more fluidly. In Buddhism, they call these master teachers that teach ways to live a life with less suffering and ascend into Buddhahood "Bodhisattvas."

Again, the definition of a "Buddha" is awakened in the game. He or she is more conscious of what they intend to create and experience in their sojourn. They have become self-aware of how the hologram self organizes to match the user's mandala observing it. Once awakening is realized by oneself, then the physical possessions, cultural status, labels of success, and other forms of 3rd-dimensional value statements no longer become highly relevant. This is because an awakened Buddha is grateful for the life he or she experiences.

Earth offers souls the ability to gain merits and level up their energy by relieving the suffering of people asking for help and raising consciousness. The Buddhas can create better experiences for themselves because they travel between parallel realities and bring only their luggage of experiences, not physical items that may or may not transfer correctly between parallel realities. Even the people that Buddhas love are parallel versions of themselves. The Buddha knows this and respects their parallel loved one's journey to evolved spiritually at their own pace while loving them as they are at that moment in this parallel reality.

Every moment is the process of creating a new expression to be experienced and a shift into a parallel version of reality that offers plenty to be grateful for. The Buddha knows that life lived in gratitude releases those Gamma brain waves that connect to the universal one mind. Connection to the universal one-mind brings more and more synchronicity to unfold in your life. As a Buddha steps towards a perspective that changes their frequency, they enter higher and higher realities full of more resonance. Every Buddha knows that there is no right or wrong way to explore parallel realities, so there are Buddhas at all dimensions of reality. No dimension is better or worse than another. Each dimension has its sweetness and opportunities for personal growth and development up the levels of consciousness.

Unfortunately, pain and suffering are often inflicted by people through their personal choices and perspectives in how they want to live their lives. Through the bottoms in people's lives, they have the opportunity to rise above the pain and suffering to choose another way to live their life in more harmony if they want to. Some people secretly enjoy pain, suffering, and unresolved dramas in their life stories. It comes down to personal choices. The Buddha sees and understands this. He or she sends love and compassion to those who suffer in their delusions in the holographic game of life. The Buddhas offer Dharma talks hoping that the wisdom resonates so that those who suffer may choose the pathway that leads to more fluid and pleasant experiences.

On the book cover, you have one such Buddha who is revered for being compassionate to people who suffer in the game of life. Kwan Yin is a famous female Buddha in China. She discovered Buddhism through the teachings of Bodhidharma in the Tibetan mountainous areas of China during her lifetime as a Chinese princess. Upon her ascension into Buddhahood, she decided to keep traveling back out of the void and beyond into the physical world to be compassionate to those that suffer in the eons.

After reading this book, you should already know how to read the meaning behind Buddhist mandalas. The book cover means this. The book cover is Kwan Yin, a female princess. She chooses to pursue Buddhahood by having her awakening and ascending the levels of consciousness into a heightened state of energy in her Merkabah. Kwan Yin reached Buddhahood in her youth and spent the rest of her life teaching dharma wisdom. In the artwork, she radiates a large halo around her head and an even larger halo around her body.

These halos are her Merkabah she travels in when she shifts between parallel realities and dimensions. The chariot she prefers is a 5th-dimensional dragon. Dragons in Asia are believed to be invisible to the 3rd dimension because they are believed to exist in a 5th-dimensional state of consciousness. Kwan Yin is legendary for revealing herself in times of distress to people who call her for help. The solutions are often guiding people to uncover their abundance blocks. In the meantime, she aids in relieving immediate suffering before she moves on. Kwan Yin is an example of a Bodhisattva, and there are legions of Bodhisattvas who reveal the structure of the game while playing in the game with you.

The famous Buddhist chant associated with Kwan Yin that I've heard thousands of times is, "Om mani padme hum." I wish for all who want to partake in a conscious and self-aware journey to become the embodiment of the chant themselves. "Om mani padme hum" means the jewel in the lotus flower is an enlightened being. The goal of each incarnation with its many lessons is for the person to reveal one leaf at a time, learn one lesson at a time, and leaf after leaf get closer to the lotus flower center. The center of the lotus flower is you. You eventually become an enlightened being. This, as do many other mantras, may lead to the sound of silence, which is the essence of non-polarity. The Lord is silent. Until then, your life lived at its best is an answered prayer to many parallel realities you visit. My intention for writing this book is to help reduce suffering. Although the path towards your enlightenment is full of challenging personal terrain, this path is only interesting to those who eventually reach it in their destiny. **Welcome to your Buddhahood.**

About the Author

Von D. Galt is an author who has studied Buddhism for the past four decades and counting. She grew up studying metaphysics, consciousness, eastern energy medicine, and Buddhist art history from her Laotian Buddhist upbringing. In ***Buddhist Mandalas: Explore Parallel Realities with Sacred Geometry***, readers worldwide get insight into the process of spiritual awakening and ascension up the levels of consciousness into Buddhahood through an introductory study of sacred geometry in Buddhist mandalas. If you enjoyed this dharma talk, then stay tuned for more dharma talks she publishes from the void and beyond into infinite love.

Index

Introduction ... 1
What is Sacred Geometry? ... 14
Sacred Geometry in Earth's Grid ... 24
Sacred Space & Ley Lines ... 48
Vesica Piscis ... 65
Flower of Life Research Leads to Metatron's Cube ... 77
Flower of Life in Language Changes DNA ... 87
Metatron's Cube ... 103
Sacred Geometry in Spirituality ... 125
Sri Yantra ... 131
Yin Yang Symbol ... 165
Tree of Life ... 183
Torus Vortex ... 199
Swastika in Indigenous Cultures ... 213
What is Consciousness? ... 232
Consciousness & Oneness ... 240
Power of the Heart ... 260
Meditation Changes Reality ... 289
Awakening & Ascension ... 321
Conclusion ... 355
About the Author ... 373
Index ... 374
Bibliography ... 375

Bibliography

ABC News. "Colorado Dark Knight Shooting Witness: I Saw A Guy Right Next to Me Getting Shot." *YouTube* video. July 20, 2012.
http://www.youtube.com/watch?v=oNcAMRAePZk

ABC News. "Sikh Temple Shooting: Domestic Terrorism." *YouTube* video. August 5, 2012.
http://www.youtube.com/watch?v=J4MZSXNAS2U

ABC News. "Trump Inauguration Speech." *YouTube* video. January 20, 2017.
https://youtu.be/sRBsJNdK1t0

Activeda. "Meditation Spiritual Yoga 1384758." Pixabay.com. Accessed 5, January, 2020.
https://pixabay.com/illustrations/meditation-spiritual-yoga-1384758/

Arenander, Ph.D., Alarik. "About Dr, Arenander." EBrainMatrix.org.
https://ebrainmatrix.org/about.html

Arni, Samhita (May 22, 2017). "Gender Doesn't Come in the Way of Nirvana." THG Publishing PVT Ltd.
https://www.thehindu.com/society/history-and-culture/samhita-arni-points-out-how-caste-and-gender-prejudice-are-inextricably-linked/article17433634.ece

Armour, J. Andrew, MD, PhD. (2007). "The Little Brain on the Heart." Cleveland Clinic Journal of Medicine, Volume (74), S48. Doi: https://www.ccjm.org/content/74/2_suppl_1/S48

Associated Press. "Pakistan Yet to Find 139 Buried in Avalanche." Fox News. Accessed November 14, 2012. https://www.foxnews.com/world/pakistan-yet-to-find-139-buried-in-avalanche

AZ Quotes, Inc. AZQuotes.com. Retrieved January 19, 2020 from https://www.azquotes.com/author/64071-Bodhidharma

AZ Quotes, Inc. AZQuotes.com. Retrieved January 19, 2020 from https://www.azquotes.com/author/4029-Dogen

AZ Quotes, Inc. AZQuotes.com. Retrieved January 21, 2020 from https://www.azquotes.com/author/26325-Mikao_Usui

Becker, Williams and Hagens, Bethe (1984). "The Planetary Grid a New Synthesis." Mission Ignition. Accessed 1, September, 2010. http://missionignition.net/bethe/planetary_grid.php

Berger Foundation. "Glossary Tao." Berger Foundation.com. Accessed 2, March, 2020. https://www.bergerfoundation.ch/glossaire/chine/glossary_tao_confu.html

Bernazzani, Sophia. "15 Great Customer Service Quotes to Inspire You." Hubspot. Accessed 25 October, 2019. https://blog.hubspot.com/service/customer-service-quotes.

Blake, Michael John. "What Pi Sounds Like". *YouTube* video. March 23, 2011. https://www.youtube.com/watch?v=YOQb_mtkEEE

Biomeridian Testing. "What is Biomeridian Testing?" Biomeridiantesting.com. https://www.biomeridiantesting.com/index.html

Book Facts. "Rig Veda is Composed at Least 23,720 BCE." BookFacts.com. Accessed 30, December, 2012. https://www.booksfact.com/vedas/rig-veda/rig-veda-is-composed-atleast-in-23720-bce.html

Buckminster Fuller Institute. "About Fuller." BFI.org. November, 2010, https://www.bfi.org/about-fuller

Buddhas Brain Channel. Hansen, Ph.D., Rick. "The Neurology of Awakening." *YouTube* video. November 11, 2011. http://www.youtube.com/watch?v=mK_ngFJWx-g

Buddha. (n.d.). BrainyQuote.com. Retrieved January 18, 2020, from BrainyQuote.com. https://www.brainyquote.com/authors/buddha-quotes

Calter, Paul (1998). "Geometry in Art & Architecture: Polygons, Tilings, & Sacred Geometry." Dartmouth University. http://www.dartmouth.edu/~matc/math5.geometry/unit5/unit5.html

Caliskan, Okan. Meditation Ego Death. Pixabay GmbH. https://pixabay.com/illustrations/meditation-ego-ego-death-3963013/

Clinton, Joseph D. "Joe Clinton: R. Buckminster Fuller's Jitterbug: Its Fascination and Some Challenges." *YouTube* video. May 23, 2011. http://www.youtube.com/watch?v=J19eV7Z1x3M

CBS Evening News. "Women's Marches Held From Coast to Coast." *YouTube* video. January 21, 2017. https://youtu.be/oLW35NrpQvo

CNN. "Highlights from Obama's Farewell Address." *YouTube* video. January 10, 2017.
https://www.youtube.com/watch?v=Zd4sSlWInuo

CNN News. "Syria Government Denies Tremseh Massacre Claim." *YouTube* video. July 15, 2012.
http://www.youtube.com/watch?v=JbHV3yKlvh4

Cody, Melissa. "Melissa Cody's Whirling Logs: Don't You Dare Call Them Swastikas". *Indian Country Today Media Network*. 7 August 2013.
https://web.archive.org/web/20130811070916/http:/indiancountrytodaymedianetwork.com/2013/08/07/melissa-codys-whirling-logs-dont-you-dare-call-them-swastikas-150782

Cymascope. "Cymatics: Harmonic Mandalas from the Human Voice". *YouTube* video. February 16, 2011.
http://www.youtube.com/watch?v=vN-n3Q9d6Q8

Department of Astronomy. "The Precession of the Earth's Axis." Cornell University. Cornell Center for Astrophysics and Planetary Science.
http://hosting.astro.cornell.edu/academics/courses/astro201/earth_precess.htm

Dictionary.com LLC (2020). "Torus." Dictionary. Accessed 3, January, 2020.
https://www.dictionary.com/browse/torus

Dictionary.com LLC (2020). "Vortex." Dictionary. Accessed 3, January, 2020.
https://www.dictionary.com/browse/vortex?s=t

Dobbs, David. (2005). Zen Gamma. Scientific American Mind. 16. 9-9. 10.1038/scientificamericanmind0405-9b. Gamma Brain Wave in Meditation.
https://www.ncbi.nlm.nih.gov/pmc/articles/PMC5261734/

Dogen. Encyclopedia Britannica. Retrieved January 21, 2020, from Britannica.com.
https://www.britannica.com/biography/Dogen

Dusen, Mel Van. "Amit Goswami: A Quantum View of God." *YouTube* video. December, 17 2008.
http://www.youtube.com/watch?v=2V6SaBflpiM&feature=relmfu

Free SVG. "Vortex Math." FreeSVG.org.
https://freesvg.org/vortex-math

F. Zeidan, K. T. Martucci, R. A. Kraft, N. S. Gordon, J. G. McHaffie, R. C. Coghill. Brain Mechanisms Supporting the Modulation of Pain by Mindfulness Meditation. *Journal of Neuroscience*, 2011; 31 (14): 5540 DOI: 10.1523/JNEUROSCI.5791-10.2011
https://www.sciencedaily.com/releases/2009/04/090427131315.htm

Garajajev, PhD., Pjotr (Peter Gariaev) and Poponin, Vladimir (1998). "DNA BioComputer Reprogramming." Rex Research.
http://www.rexresearch.com/gajarev/gajarev.htm

Gilchrist, Charles. "Sacred Geometry." *YouTube* video. October, 25, 2009.
https://www.youtube.com/channel/UC7R6AP2RCH_vRgDxFhxo3vw

Gilchrist, Charles. "Sacred Geometry: Pi, Phi, Fibonacci Sequence." *YouTube* video. February 11, 2011. http://www.youtube.com/watch?v=12m1FPheZa0&feature=related

Global Consciousness Project (1999). "What is the Nature of Global Consciousness?" Princeton University. http://noosphere.princeton.edu/

Goldman, Jonathan. "Project Om Chart." HealingSounds.com. Accessed 2012. http://www.healingsounds.com/sounds/project_om_chart.asp

Hagelin, MD, PhD., John (2007). "The Power of the Collective." Shift: At the Frontiers of Consciousness. No. 15, June-August 2007. http://istpp.org/pdf/Shift-PoweroftheCollective.pdf

Hanh, Thich Nhat. "I See You In Me and Me In You Interbeing with Thich Nhat Hanh." *YouTube* video. July, 12, 2017. https://www.youtube.com/watch?time_continue=2&v=4VFMqIZevts&feature=emb_logo

Hanson, PhD., Rick (2008, October 4). "The Evolution and Transcendence of Self." AudioDharma.org. https://www.audiodharma.org/teacher/70/

Hanson, PhD., Rick (2007, December 1). "The Neurology of Awakening." AudioDharma.org. https://www.audiodharma.org/teacher/70/

Hammond, Elizabeth. "3D Sri Yantra Alternating Merkaba Vector Equilibrium." Pinterest.com. Accessed 5, January, 2020. https://www.pinterest.com/pin/447967494157672822/

Haramein, Nassim (2018). "Physics Aether Units – The Torus & Nassim Haramein." Cosmic-core.org. https://www.cosmic-core.org/free/article-102a-science-aether-units-part-6-the-torus-nassim-haramein/

Haramein, Nassim. "Resonance Science Foundation." Resonance Science. https://resonancescience.org/

Hawkins, MD, PhD., David R. (2012). "Power Vs. Force." Veritas Publishing. https://veritaspub.com/product/power-vs-force-the-hidden-determinants-of-human-behavior/

Heartmath Institute. "Global Coherence Monitoring System." Heartmath.org. Accessed August 16, 2011. http://www.glcoherence.org/monitoring-sys.../about-system.html

Heartmath Institute. "Global Coherence Live Data." Heartmath.org. Accessed August 16, 2010. http://www.glcoherence.org/monitoring-system/live-data.html

Heath, PhD., Wallace G. (2003). "Some Biophysical Bases for the Human Energy System." Energetic Fitness. http://www.energeticfitness.com/Support%20Files/Some%20Biophysical%20Bases%20for%20the%20Human%20Energy%20System.pdf

Heartmath Institute. Heartmath. Heartmath.org. September, 2010, https://www.heartmath.org/

Heartmath Institute. "Global Coherance." Heartmath.org. Accessed August 16, 2011. https://www.heartmath.org/research/global-coherence/

Heartmath Institute. "Magnetic Field of the Heart." Heartmath.org. https://www.heartmath.org/assets/uploads/2009/09/HMI-Blog-Each-Individual-Impacts-the-Field-Environment.jpg

Henry, Charles R. (2000). "Sacred Geometry New Discoveries Linking the Great Pyramids to the Human Form." Department of Sculpture Virginia Commonwealth University. http://www.people.vcu.edu/~chenry/?fbclid=IwAR2pR76LHpKMJQUjF5h2trcE2tLJiesE0iHL2k10O1WFSKKXtuEP2y6Ed7g

Infinite Wisdom Channel. "Alan Watts – How to See Through the Game." *YouTube* video. February 12, 2017. https://youtu.be/_h-FswIACKE

Institute of Noetic Sciences. "Getting the Love You Want with Harville Hendrix." Institute of Noetic Sciences Digital Media Library. http://library.noetic.org/library/audio-teleseminars/getting-love-you-want-harville-hendrix

International Association of Reiki Practitioners. "History of Reiki." IARP, Accessed 21 January, 2020. https://iarp.org/history-of-reiki/.

Jansch, Boris. "Chartres Cathedral: Sacred Geometry." *YouTube* video. November, 2011. http://www.youtube.com/watch?v=NeGdvTgROfw&feature=results_video&playnext=1&list=PL86529E1495E0BB72

Jarus, Owen (December 20, 2012). "Abydos: Egyptian Tombs & Cult of Osiris." Live Science. Future US, Inc. https://www.livescience.com/25738-abydos.html

Keefe, Brian. "Global Consciousness Project". CBS2 News. *YouTube* video. July 28, 2008.
http://www.youtube.com/watch...

Khanna, Madhu (1979). "Yantra: The Tantric Symbol of Cosmic Unity." Thames and Hudson Publishing.
https://sriyantraresearch.com/Yantra/yantra.html?fbclid=IwA R3Nwsjp-r3cOn_WIU37kT8FjEKmroHTu1muGzSORrIIdZwgFja2Y3ZUXYY

Koch, John. "Sacred Geometry in Building." Labyrinth.net. au. Accessed 10, December, 2010.
http://www.labyrinth.net.au/~jkoch/sacred.html

Kulaichev, Alexey Pavlovich (2011). "Sri Yantra and Its Mathematical Properties." Biology Faculty of Moscow University Moscow USSR.
https://sriyantraresearch.com/References/Kulaichev%20Addi tion.pdf?fbclid=IwAR3TVRI6BR2YK6BG2kwqeCc1657Vt_MSw x2m3VL5EbXRUJS4dKbTNnP7L3U

Loken, Camillo (2009). "Brainwaves." One-Mind-One-Energy.com.
https://www.one-mind-one-energy.com/brainwaves.html

Loken, Camillo (2009). "Multiverses." One-Mind-One-Energy.com.
http://www.one-mind-one-energy.com/multiverse.html

MacDonald, Fiona (November 3, 2015). "NASA Can't Explain Who Made These Huge, 8,000-Year0Old Structures in Kazakhstan." ScienceAlert.com.
https://www.sciencealert.com/nasa-can-t-explain-who-made-these-huge-8-000-year-old-glyphs-in-kazakhstan

Mathologer Patreon. "Times Tables, Mandelbrot and the Heart of Mathematics." *YouTube* video. November 6, 2015. https://www.youtube.com/watch?v=qhbuKbxJsk8

Mindshock TV Series (2006). "Mindshock: Transplanting Memories?" Channel 4 UK. Accessed 20 October, 2008. https://www.imdb.com/title/tt0824054/

Montalk. "Earth Grid Research." Montalk.net. June, 2006, http://montalk.net/science/115/earth-grid-research

NASA/JPL-Caltech/ESA, the Hubble Heritage Team (STScI/AURA) (January 16, 1996). "Hubble Finds an Hourglass Nebula Around a Dying Star." Nasa Jet Propulsion Laboratory California Institute of Technology.
https://www.jpl.nasa.gov/spaceimages/details.php?id=PIA14442

Nelson, Roger (2011, January 16). "Detecting Mass Consciousness: Effects of Globally Shared Attention and Emotion." Journal of Cosmology.
http://noosphere.princeton.edu/papers/pdf/detectmasswithfigs.pdf?fbclid=IwAR0pqVItYgdnXjf0t6tVTqKNJDSXJP1p3qWNzfyGl-tCkR-GK2bujmkKma4

Nelson, Roger and Bancel, Peter (2008, March 14). "The GCP Event Experiment: Design, Analytical Methods, Results." Noosphere.Princeton.edu.
http://noosphere.princeton.edu/papers/pdf/GCP.Events.Mar08.prepress.pdf?fbclid=IwAR057pqm6WDmtp-9oOTpaSVSdmT75Fre-qEDzzAA4xKwWzcwNlH8JNkcExM

Olympic Channel. "Olympics Opening Ceremony." *YouTube* video. July 27, 2012.
http://www.youtube.com/watch?v=dk-sDskIFeQ

Omega 432. "Cymatics Music." Omega432.com.
http://www.omega432.com/music.html

Pettis, Chuck (1998). "The Seattle Ley-Line Map." The Geo Group.
http://www.geo.org/qa.htm#tof

Pixabay. "Human Faces Personal Connected 977414." Pixabay.com. Accessed 5, January, 2020.
https://pixabay.com/illustrations/human-faces-personal-connected-977414/

Plum Village. "A Collective Awakening for the Future of Our Planet." PlumVillage.org.
http://www.plumvillage.org/video/238-a-collective-awakening-for-the-future-of-our-planet.html

Popiotek, Stephen (2011). "Spiritual Exploration – Kabbalah: The Tree of Life." Accessed 5, July, 2011.
https://sites.google.com/site/stephenpopiotek/

Popp, Fritz-Albert (2018). "Professor Fritz-Albert Popp." International Union of Medical and Applied Bioelectrography.
https://www.iumab.org/prof-fritz-albert-popp/

Powell, Randy (2018). "The Grand Unified Field Theory – The Language of God." The Other Side of Midnight.
https://www.theothersideofmidnight.com/20180930-powell/

Powell, Randy. "Randy Powell: Intro to Vortex Math." *YouTube* video. December, 22, 2010.
http://www.youtube.com/watch?v=Fbyc9JW3vtk

Powell, Randy. "Vortex Math." Accessed 10, July, 2011.
http://www.vortexmath.com/

Proven Cal Voice (2010). "Sri Yantra Om." Provencalvoice.com.
https://www.provencalvoice.com/sri-yantra-om/

PX Fuel. "Free Photo Jangr." PXFuel.com. Accessed 5, January, 2020.
https://www.pxfuel.com/en/free-photo-jangr

PX Fuel. "Free Photo Qnrfg." PXFuel.com. Accessed 5, January, 2020.
https://www.pxfuel.com/en/free-photo-qnrfg

Red, John Stuart and Baker, Dean (2013). "Harmonic Voice Mandalas." Cymascope.com. Sonic Age America, Llc.
https://www.cymascope.com/shop/wp-content/uploads/2013/08/Harmonic_Voice_Mandala.pdf

Rice, Michael. "Holistic House Plans." Holistic House Plans.
http://www.holistichouseplans.com/

Rightful Place in Creation." CymaticSource.com.
http://www.cymaticsource.com/pdf/QuestersArticle.pdf

Satyana Institute. "13 Principles of Spiritual Progression." SpiritPortal.org.
https://www.spiritportal.org/thirteen-principles-of-spiritual-activism.html

Schiavone, Christine. "Spiritual Exploration: Kabbalah." *YouTube* video. October 30, 2011.
http://www.youtube.com/watch?v=s_603OiA21E&feature=endscreen&NR=1

Shah, Bipin R. "Swastika Was Used in Neolithic, Bronze and Iron Age Cultures and Its Probable Origin is from Astrology." Academia.edu. Accessed 10, February, 2010. https://www.academia.edu/11165695/Swastika_was_used_in_Neolithic_Bronze_and_Iron_Age_cultures_and_its_probable_origin_is_from_Astrology

Silva, Freddy. "The Practical Magic of Sacred Space." *YouTube* video. November, 2011.
http://www.youtube.com/watch?v=uBnagFJ5bgc

Simmons, PhD., Geoffrey (November, 2008). "Sacred Spaces and Sacred Places." University of Calgary.
http://dspace.ucalgary.ca/bitstream/1880/46834/1/Sacred%20Spaces.pdf

Stevens, John (2007). "What is an Enso?" Lion's Roar Foundation.
https://www.lionsroar.com/what-is-an-enso/

Snelson, Kenneth. "Tensegrity to Weaving Transformation." *YouTube* video. July 8, 2009.
https://youtu.be/zYYulzfegzs

Snelson, Kenneth (2012). "Tensegrity, Weaving and the Binary World." KennethSnelson.net.
http://kennethsnelson.net/Tensegrity_and_Weaving.pdf

Sosa, Joshua. "Joshua Sosa Presentation." Acupuncture and Massage School.
http://s3.amazonaws.com/libapps/accounts/55065/images/Joshua_Sosa_presentation_image.gif

Sri Yantra Research Center (2012). "Solving the Sri Yantra." SriYantraResearchCenter.com. https://sriyantraresearch.com/Optimal/optimal_sri_yantra.htm?fbclid=IwAR1uSLUuG_sAPTtIWX2ll4ekuoPHBSB_ZkbIbL5AHQMvzSDul5c-3LqUMbU

Tsakiris, Alex (April 28). "Dr. Peter Bancel Assists Goldsmiths, University of London with Global Consciousness Project." Skeptiko Science at the Tipping Point. Skeptiko.com. https://skeptiko.com/peter-bancel-global-consciousness-project/?fbclid=IwAR2yxydN4fJIMHzxMjVjPkbwElEgxI-I-F_wHepw80WFp3FJBhBaaZHunkE

The Guardian News. "Somalia Theatre Suicide Bombing Kills Top Sports Officials." The Guardian. Accessed April 4, 2012. https://www.theguardian.com/world/2012/apr/04/somalia-theatre-suicide-bombing?fbclid=IwAR3oE87OtVYrokf_UrfwCkLIC2Lj8PNLUDzb7e3dW6rY2-BXenfIpcz3urM

The New York Times and the Los Angeles Times. "More Than 350 Trapped, Die in Honduras Prison Inferno." The Seattle Times. https://www.seattletimes.com/nation-world/more-than-350-trapped-die-in-honduras-prison-inferno/

The Global Consciousness Project. "Overall Summary of Results August 1998 to December 2015." Princeton University. http://noosphere.princeton.edu/results.html

Thelema Press (2006). "Sex: The Secret Gate to Eden." Thelema Press Productions. https://www.imdb.com/title/tt0947072/

Thrive (2011). "Thrive: What on Earth Will It Take?" ThriveMovement.com. https://www.imdb.com/title/tt2063834/?ref_=ttqt_qt_tt

Times USA LLC. "Oakland Massacre: Shooter Kills Seven at Christian Nursing School." Time.com. http://www.time.com/.../nation/article/0,8599,2110909,00.html...

Unikolom (November 20, 2019). "Aryans: The Founders of Vedic Civilization." Unikolom.com. https://unikolom.com/aryans-the-founders-of-vedic-civilization-vedic-period-vedic-literature/

Unikolom (December 11, 2019). "Vedic Sanskit: The Computer Language of Vedic Period." Unikolom.com. https://unikolom.com/vedic-sanskrit-the-computer-language-of-vedic-period/

Veritas Publishing. "David R. Hawkins, MD, PhD." VeritasPub.com. Accessed 3, August, 2009. https://veritaspub.com/dr-hawkins/

Vey, Gary (2010). "Is DNA the Next Internet? Are Humans Really Beings of Light?" ViewZone.com. http://www.viewzone.com/dnax.html

Volk, Jeff. "Vibration to Manifestation: Assuming Our Heartmath Institute. "Global Coherance." Heartmath.org. Accessed August 16, 2011.

Wang, Chuanxin, MD. (2019). "Yin-Yang in Traditional Chinese Medicine." Acupuncture and Massage College. https://www.amcollege.edu/blog/yin-and-yang-in-traditional-chinese-medicine

Wake Forest Baptist Medical Center. (2011, April 11). Demystifying meditation: Brain imaging illustrates how meditation reduces pain. *Science Daily*. Retrieved April 14, 2020 from www.sciencedaily.com/releases/2011/04/110405174835.htm

War Paths 2 Peace Pipes. "Native American Symbols – Swastika." Accessed 3, November, 2011.
https://www.warpaths2peacepipes.com/native-american-symbols/swastika-symbol.htm

Weber, Daniel, PhD., MSc. "The Yin Yang Nature of Immunity." *YouTube* video. November 3, 2009.
http://www.youtube.com/watch?v=BwP2Kggilmo

Whitmire, Tiffney. "Sacred Places: Sacred Geo." Sweet Briar College.
http://www.arthistory.sbc.edu/sacredplaces/sacredgeo.html

Wikimedia Foundation, Inc. "Alfred Watkins." Wikimedia. Accessed 30, January, 2020.
https://en.wikipedia.org/wiki/Alfred_Watkins

Wikimedia Foundation, Inc. "Mandala." Wikimedia. Accessed 18, January, 2020.
https://en.wikipedia.org/wiki/Mandala.

Wikimedia Foundation, Inc. "Metatron." Wikimedia. Accessed 12, July, 2019.
https://en.wikipedia.org/wiki/Metatron

Wikimedia Foundation, Inc. "Overlapping Circles." Wikimedia. Accessed 1, January, 2011.
https://en.wikipedia.org/wiki/Overlapping_circles_grid#Modern_usage

Wikimedia Foundation, Inc. "Cluny Coffret Christ." Wikimedia. Accessed 6, March, 2006.
https://commons.wikimedia.org/wiki/File:CLUNY-Coffret_Christ_1.JPG

Wikimedia Foundation, Inc. "Heart Field." Wikimedia. Accessed 14, November, 2012.
https://commons.wikimedia.org/wiki/File:Heart-field.jpg

Wikimedia Foundation, Inc. "Plasmas Sphere." Wikimedia. Accessed 15, June, 2009.
https://commons.wikimedia.org/wiki/File:Plasmasphere.jpg

Wikimedia Foundation, Inc. "Barry Kerzin Meditating with EEG for Neuroscience Research." Wikimedia. Accessed 8, March, 2017.
https://commons.wikimedia.org/wiki/File:Barry_Kerzin_meditating_with_EEG_for_neuroscience_research.jpg

Wikimedia Foundation, Inc. "Eckhart Tolle, the Dalai Lama and Ken Robinson at Vancouver." Wikimedia. Accessed 26, September, 2009.
https://commons.wikimedia.org/wiki/File:Eckhart_Tolle,_the_Dalai_Lama_and_Ken_Robinson_at_Vancouver.jpg

Wikimedia Foundation, Inc. "The Vedas." Wikimedia. Accessed 15, June, 2007.
https://en.wikibooks.org/wiki/Hinduism/The_Vedas

Wikimedia Foundation, Inc. "Temple of Osiris Flower of Life." Wikimedia. Accessed 5, January, 2014.
https://commons.wikimedia.org/wiki/File:Temple-of-Osiris_Flower-of-Life_02.jpg

Wikimedia Foundation, Inc. "China Beijing Forbidden City." Wikimedia. Accessed 9, January, 2014.
https://en.wikipedia.org/wiki/File:China-beijing-forbidden-city-P1000157-detail.jpg

Wikimedia Foundation, Inc. "Floor Decorations from the Palace of King Ashurbanipal." Wikimedia. Accessed 18, September, 2011.
https://en.wikipedia.org/wiki/File:Floor_decoration_from_the_palace_of_King_Ashurbanipal.jpg

Wikimedia Foundation, Inc. "Mosaic Floor from a Bathhouse in Herod." Wikimedia. Accessed 16, November, 2012.
https://en.wikipedia.org/wiki/File:Mosaic_floor_from_a_bathhouse_in_Herod%27s_palace_-_Google_Art_Project.jpg

Wikimedia Foundation, Inc. "Swatiska." Wikimedia. Accessed 9, August, 2014.
https://en.wikipedia.org/wiki/Swastika

Wikimedia Foundation, Inc. "Metatron's Solids." Wikimedia. Accessed 4, April, 2012.
https://commons.wikimedia.org/wiki/File:Metatron_solids.svg

Wikimedia Foundation, Inc. "Carboxysome 3." Wikimedia. Accessed 4, September, 2008.
https://commons.wikimedia.org/wiki/File:Carboxysome_3_images-en.svg

Wikimedia Foundation, Inc. "Caduceus as a Symbol of Medicine." Wikimedia. Accessed 20, July, 2011.
http://en.wikipedia.org/wiki/Caduceus_as_a_symbol_of_medicine

Wikimedia Foundation, Inc. "Bhutanese Thangka of Mt. Meru and the Buddhist Universe." Wikimedia. Accessed 13, February, 2008.
https://commons.wikimedia.org/wiki/File:Bhutanese_thanka_of_Mt._Meru_and_the_Buddhist_Universe.jpg

Wikimedia Foundation, Inc. "Hertz." Wikimedia. Accessed 11, February, 2008.
https://en.wikipedia.org/wiki/Hertz

Wikimedia Foundation, Inc. "Merkabah Mysticism." Wikimedia. Accessed 12, March, 2012.
https://en.wikipedia.org/wiki/Merkabah_mysticism

Wikimedia Foundation, Inc. "Tree of Life." Wikimedia. Accessed 10, January, 2011.
http://en.wikipedia.org/wiki/Tree_of_life

Wikimedia Foundation, Inc. "Shakyamuni Buddha with Avadana Legend Scenes." Wikimedia. Accessed 19, June, 2019.
https://upload.wikimedia.org/wikipedia/commons/d/da/Shakyamuni_Buddha_with_Avadana_Legend_Scenes_-_Google_Art_Project.jpg

Wikimedia Foundation, Inc. "Kwan Yin Exhibition Inheriting Intangible Culture Heritage Regong." Wikimedia. Accessed 13, November, 2019.
https://commons.wikimedia.org/wiki/File:HKCL_%E9%A6%99%E6%B8%AF%E4%B8%AD%E5%A4%AE%E5%9C%96%E6%9B%B8%E9%A4%A8_CWB_%E5%B1%95%E8%A6%BD_exhibition_Inheriting_Intangible_Culture_Heritage_Regong_%E5%94%90%E5%8D%A1_Thangka_November_2019_SS2_05.jpg

Wikimedia Foundation, Inc. "Shakyamuni Thangka." Wikimedia. Accessed 23, February, 2017.
https://commons.wikimedia.org/wiki/File:Shakyamuni-Thangka.jpg

Wikimedia Foundation, Inc. "Kagyu Refuge Tree." Wikimedia. Accessed 1, January, 2011.
https://commons.wikimedia.org/wiki/File:KagyuRefugeTree.jpg

Wikimedia Foundation, Inc. "Mongolia White Tara." Wikimedia. Accessed 14, July, 2014.
https://commons.wikimedia.org/wiki/File:Mongolia_White_Tara.jpg

Wikimedia Foundation, Inc. "Black Hole Continuum and Its Gravity Well." Wikimedia. Accessed 5, September, 2017.
https://commons.wikimedia.org/wiki/File:Black-hole_continuum_and_its_gravity_well.png

Wikimedia Foundation, Inc. "Zazen Bell with Enso in Background." Wikimedia. Accessed 7, March, 2010.
https://commons.wikimedia.org/wiki/File:Zazen_bell_with_Enso_in_Background.jpg

Wikimedia Foundation, Inc. "Arabic Numeral System." Wikimedia. Accessed 9, March, 2020.
https://en.wikipedia.org/wiki/Hindu%E2%80%93Arabic_numeral_system

Wikimedia Foundation, Inc. "Nakshatra." Wikimedia. Accessed 25, March, 2020.
https://en.wikipedia.org/wiki/Nakshatra

Wikimedia Foundation, Inc. "Faraday Wave." Wikiwand. Accessed 29, July, 2012.
https://www.wikiwand.com/en/Faraday_wave

Wikimedia Foundation, Inc. "Swatiska." Wikimedia. Accessed 17, May, 2010.
https://en.wikipedia.org/wiki/Swastika

Wikimedia Foundation, Inc. "Lunar Station." Wikimedia. Accessed 15, October, 2011.
https://en.wikipedia.org/wiki/Lunar_station

Wikimedia Foundation, Inc. "Mound Builders." Wikimedia. Accessed 2, November, 2010.
https://en.wikipedia.org/wiki/Mound_Builders

Wikimedia Foundation, Inc. "Tara Buddhism." Wikimedia. Accessed 7, March, 2010.
https://en.wikipedia.org/wiki/Tara_(Buddhism)

Zandi, Roya, Reguera, David, Bruinsma, Robijn F., Gelbart, William M., and Rusnick, Joseph (November, 2, 2004). "Origin of Icosahedral Symmetry in Viruses." Proceedings of the National Academy of Sciences of the United States of America. Vol. 101. No. 44.
https://www.pnas.org/content/pnas/101/44/15556.full.pdf

Made in United States
Troutdale, OR
10/29/2024

24050190R00246